YOUR
ROAD TO
RECOVERY

ORAL
ROBERTS

A Division of Th_____
Nashville • Atlanta • Camden • New York

Second printing

Published in Nashville, Tennessee, by Oliver-Nelson Books, a division of Thomas Nelson, Inc., Publishers, and distributed in Canada by Lawson Falle, Ltd., Cambridge, Ontario.

Unless otherwise noted, Bible verses used in this publication are from the NEW KING JAMES VERSION. Copyright © 1979, 1980, 1982 by Thomas Nelson, Inc., Publishers.

Printed in the United States of America.

Library of Congress Cataloging-in-Publication Data

Roberts, Oral.
    Your road to recovery.

    1. Spiritual healing. I. Title.
BT732.5.R59   1986   248.4   86-5157
ISBN 0-8407-9058-9

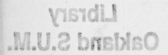

YOUR
ROAD TO
RECOVERY

Dedication

*To my parents, Ellis Melvin and Claudius
Priscilla Roberts, who are now in heaven and
who first put me on the road to recovery—a road
that once discovered must always be followed day
after day, week after week, year after year, until
that final moment when we leave this earth to go
to our heavenly home where there's always
everything we've ever dreamed and longed for.
And from that heavenly home in the NOW of
our personal lives, each of us can draw from that
inexhaustible power of wholeness spiritually,
physically, and financially and wholeness in our
relationships with one another—and know that
we know we can WIN!*

*Their son,
Oral*

Contents

Personal Acknowledgments

To my darling wife, Evelyn, who said, "Oral, you've got to write this book for there are so many who will recover if they can catch your spirit, get hold of the formula, and work it so it will work for them . . ."

To Rebecca, Ronnie, Richard, and Roberta, my four children—two in heaven and two on earth— who from their birth have been the bright lights in my life . . .

To Jan Dargatz, Ph.D., graduate of Oral Roberts University and the University of Southern California, head of communications of the Oral Roberts Ministries, who like Evelyn "goaded" me to write this book and whose editorial help made me write better than I can write . . .

To Oliver-Nelson, my publisher, who asked me to write this book . . .

And to *you*, my reader, the most important person in the world with whom I share what I know and have experienced about Your Road to Recovery . . .

God bless you today even beyond your hopes and dreams.

You CAN Recover

Has something bad happened?

Have you been struck from your blind side with a force that has left you reeling, barely hanging on?

Is it illness?

Has the bottom dropped out of your finances?

Is your marriage breaking up? Or has it already collapsed, leaving you with the hurt and devastation of divorce?

Has a relationship with your children or parents brought you to an emotional breaking point?

Are you feeling all knotted up inside over guilt, worry, bitterness, rejection?

Are you lonelier than you've ever felt in your life?

Well . . .

I have good news for you today.

You can recover.

With God's help, you can turn this negative situation around and come out with a miracle!

"But," you say, "you don't know how low I am, Oral Roberts. You don't know how desperate my situation really is."

I may not know the specifics of what you're facing, but I know a great deal about the things the devil can throw at you.

"Like what?" you ask.

Like sickness, and the fact that I nearly lost my life to tuberculosis when I was just seventeen years old. And since then,

I've been in the hospital seven times, facing serious surgery on more than one occasion.

Like death in the family—the tragedies of losing a daughter in a plane crash and a son to suicide.

Like divorce, which my younger son faced and came through in a miraculous way.

Like broken relationships, such as the one I had with my parents before I ran away from home as a teenager.

Like being out of money so many times I've lost count of them. Like facing the challenge of receiving enough money to keep God's work going month after month after month.

Yes . . .

I know a little about something bad happening in your life.

I also know about *something good* that can happen to turn the negatives around and get you moving on the road to recovery.

The fact is . . .

I'm alive today and healthier in my body than I've ever been.

I've learned how to work through the tragedies that have struck our family . . . and to emerge stronger and more alive in my faith than before.

My darling wife, Evelyn, and I have been married forty-eight years, and we're still in love. Our remaining children, Richard and Roberta, are active in the ministry with us.

I have the greatest group of partners in the world. They have stood with me in building Oral Roberts University and the City of Faith Health-Care Center in Tulsa, Oklahoma. They have done what no comparable group of people on earth has ever done.

And we haven't stopped yet! We're still moving on for God.

"But," you say, "you're special."

No, I'm not. What God has done in my life, He can do in your life. Oh, His methods may be different to fit your circumstances and needs. He may speak to you in ways He doesn't speak to me. He may call you to do something He hasn't called me to do. But God is God. He changes not. He is in the miracle-working, recovery business! And He has miracles of recovery for you.

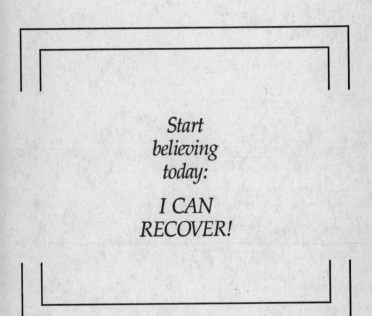

*Start
believing
today:*

*I CAN
RECOVER!*

"How can I recover?" you ask.

Well, let me share several things with you that you need to know at the very outset of this book.

First, each of us needs healing of something in our lives. Everybody is sick in some way.

Everybody wishes something could be better.

Everybody has been struck by something bad in life . . . an accident, a disease, a divorce or other broken relationship, a painful memory, a financial setback.

Everybody continues to have needs. Just when you think you've got one need met or one problem solved, another one crops up. That's just the way life is.

Consider for a moment the word *disease*—"dis-ease," "not at ease." Something is out of harmony, out of order, out of balance.

In the Bible, the word *save* includes the concept of healing. God sees your life as a *whole*, not in segments with your spirit over here, your body over there, and your relationships someplace else. If one area of your life is in trouble, then your entire life is no longer whole, and you are in a position of needing healing, saving, restoring . . . *wholeness!* To be whole means to be put back into harmony, back into order, back into balance. It is the opposite of disease.

Second, God doesn't heal everybody in the same way. Of that fact I'm certain. I've laid hands on more than a million people in my life, not counting those who have heard me preach and pray over radio or television during the last thirty-eight years. Sometimes in my crusade services I would pray for several hundred people in one night or in one afternoon—a few times more than a thousand in a day. And it is out of that commitment of my life and out of my experiences that I've come to these conclusions about healing.

Some people are instantly restored to complete wholeness by God—or their healings come very quickly, in a matter of minutes. Others are healed over a longer period of time—maybe weeks or months.

Healing is a *recovery* process. It happens *over time.*

Third, there is a difference between an instant burst of healing and the process of healing.

Almost every healing I've ever experienced personally and every healing I've seen in someone else has been a *process* of healing. Most people don't get sick or defeated or bankrupt or divorced because of what happens in a single day. We get down over a period of time. The same is true for recovery. It happens over a period of time.

What about an *instant burst* of healing?

There are two important things about an instant burst of healing. One is that every process of healing has an instant burst of healing within it. It's embedded there along the way almost like a seed is planted in the earth. There is a turnaround point. That's the instant burst of healing.

Let me give you an example.

Let's suppose you are going down a road toward a place named Sickness. You're traveling along and then something happens to cause you to make a U-turn right there in the middle of the road. Now you find yourself going in the opposite direction toward a place named Wellness. That's what I mean by an instant burst of healing. It's that one split second when things start moving away from bad and toward good.

Your instant burst of healing may not be anything you can see with your eyes. It may be the moment when the chemotherapy takes hold in your body and begins to win over the cancer cells. It may be the moment when a spark of love comes alive again in your heart . . . or a bill is fully paid . . . or something totally invisible happens that you aren't even aware of with your five senses.

The other important thing is that a burst of healing comes at the point when your *faith* really hits your *circumstances* and causes something to happen.

An instant burst of healing is something you *believe* for. It's a faith act. A process of healing is something you *do* and keep on doing. You have to make the process happen. There are principles of God at work in the healing process, and this book deals with those very principles.

Finally, recovery takes effort. It isn't always easy.

Getting the answer to your problem has to become the most important thing in your life. You've got to start saying and thinking, "I will lick this thing. I won't give up." Say it with some iron in your spine and determination in your eye. If you're willing to do that and mean it, this book can help you.

"But," you say, "don't you preach miracles?"

I know what you're thinking because I've faced that reaction many times.

You're thinking that Oral Roberts is that guy preaching miracles and that when I lay my hands on people and pray for them I expect them to walk away 100 percent well and never look back. Is that right?

Well, let me tell you how it really is.

Yes, I believe in miracles. I believe in receiving a new miracle every day! I'm expecting miracles from God all the time.

But miraculous doesn't mean instantaneous. It's just as much a miracle to me if you get well from cancer in five months as it is if you get well in five minutes. It's just as much a miracle to me if your marriage is restored through weeks of counseling as it is if you fall in love again suddenly and unexplainably.

That's because God is the Healer. He sets the timetable for your recovery. He does the healing work inside you. I don't. No doctor or counselor does the healing. God heals, and God alone heals.

What we can do is to put ourselves into the best position possible for God to work.

How do we do that? That's what I want to share with you in this book.

First, you have to deal God personally into your life. You have to count Him in on your healing.

Do you see God as a healing God? Or do you think of Him as a God of justice, sitting on His throne up in heaven, ready to punish you for every mistake you make, trying to whip you into shape and ready to throw you into hell if you fail?

That's not the God Oral Roberts knows. The God I know is a

loving, *good* God who is on your side and who wants you to be well and whole even more than *you* want to be whole.

Second, you have to take charge of your recovery and do your part.

Your recovery is a *partnership* between you and God. You can't do God's part. God won't do your part. There's an old saying that goes:

> Without God, I cannot;
> But without me, God will not.

You've got to shoulder your part of the load. Now you can't do it all, but nobody else can do your part. I can't do your part. The government can't do your part. Your spouse or child can't do your part. Your best friend can't do your part. *You* must do your part.

Think of your recovery as a project that you and God are undertaking together.

And finally, you have to really want to recover.

"Of course," you say, "I want to recover. Doesn't everybody who is down want to get back up?"

Not all the people I know. And that's not what doctors and other people tell me.

A lot of people would rather be miserable than make the effort to get well. They get into the habit of having their problem. They get used to talking about it. They get used to thinking about it. And when it comes right down to it, they get comfortable with the problem. Oh, they may complain about it all the time. They may talk a lot about how they wish they didn't have the problem they've got. But when it comes right down to it, they're more willing to live with the problem than make the effort to get rid of it. It's almost as if they're scared about what might happen if the problem was gone. So it's a very serious thing to make the decision to recover and then act on it.

Let me ask you today:

Do you *really* want to quit thinking about that thing that makes you fearful or guilty?

18

Do you *really* want to put the divorce completely behind you and get on with your life?

Do you *really* want to get out of that sickbed, even if it means having to face some of the chores and problems of life?

Do you *really* want to get out from under that mountain of bills that has you nearly buried, even if it means working harder than you've ever worked in your life?

Are you willing to risk being well and whole?

Are you sick and tired of feeling sick and tired?

Are you so fed up with being without enough money that you'll try God's way of solving the problem?

Are you weary of thinking the same old thoughts over and over again like some broken record?

Are you willing to *do something* to make your miracle happen?

Are you answering "Yes"?

Good.

Let's begin.

I believe you can make it.

I believe you can get the answer you need.

I believe you can defeat this thing that has hold of you.

I've seen it happen.

No matter how bad your situation . . . no matter how hopeless others see you . . . no matter your social class, race, age, sex, or conditions . . . I believe *you can recover*.

Your best days can still lie ahead!

Let me share with you the principles of recovery that God has for you today. . . .

Consider

1. What is keeping *you* from wholeness? What miracle do you need in your life? Name your most pressing needs and desires.

2. How do you describe God's personality? How do you believe God feels about you? Why?

3. Why is it that many people would rather *cope* with their problems than *solve* them?

4. What role do you expect God to take in *your* recovery process?

5. What do you *really* want your life to be like?

Count God In

I grew up in a home in which both my mother and my father came to trust in God, and they taught me about God while I was still just a boy. But either I caused myself to ignore Him or I just flatly "dumbed out."

How did this happen?

Well, let me say first that I was a little older than my years. I was a fast bloomer. By the time I was seventeen, I was going on thirty. And I got it into my head to get out of my parents' lives and away from the teachings of God and the Bible. I wanted to get out into the big unknown and find a place where I could follow my own dreams and make them happen.

What did I dream about?

I wanted someday to be a lawyer . . . and then a judge . . . and then the governor of the state of Oklahoma. (I was dreaming of being governor, but my chances were slim and none, and slim had just ridden out of my little town.)

I wanted to get away from the poverty of my dead-end life out in the hills of Oklahoma.

I wanted to get an education—to get through college and on to a doctor's degree. And back then, especially back *there*, folks didn't think much about college.

I wanted to be an athlete.

"Now," you may say, "that's the most normal thing in the

world for a seventeen-year-old boy to leave home and begin to work on making those dreams happen."

And it's true, there was nothing wrong with my leaving home at seventeen, *if* that was what I was supposed to do. There was nothing wrong with my dreams, *if* they were what I was supposed to do in my life.

There was something wrong, though, about my attitude and about how I planned to go after those dreams. I had left out God.

I ignored God as a fact of my existence in my daily life. I left Him out of my dreams. I failed to understand the most basic of all basic facts: *God is God*.

And God has to be dealt with. He's there. He isn't going away. You have to count Him in or count Him out.

I left home. I gave my best shot to my dreams. I ran away from Ada, Oklahoma, to a neighboring town and entered school there. I was the tallest man and the highest scorer on the basketball team in that school. Soon I was the captain, the one to lead the team. I moved in with a judge, and in the evenings I read his law books while I was still going to high school. I got a job at the little newspaper in that town, writing a column and delivering papers, so I could make some money. I was determined to make life happen.

I'd get up at 4:00 A.M., build the fires in the judge's house, go to school, practice basketball, throw my papers on my route, write my newspaper column, and maybe even have a date. Then I'd come home to study. I pushed myself to the very limits. I was earning A's. I was elected "king" of my school. I was making money. I was part of a winning team. *Nothing* was going to stop Oral Roberts!

But something did.

I began to have chest pains and to wake up in the night with severe sweats. I tired easily.

And in the midst of the final game of the district basketball tournament, I collapsed . . . bleeding at my nostrils, my lungs feeling as if they were going to burst from my body. I slipped into unconsciousness. The next thing I knew, my coach had me

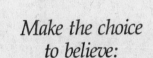

*Make the choice
to believe:*

*God is real.
God is on my side.
God is concerned about MY need.
God wants me to recover!*

lying in the backseat of his car. I heard him say words I had planned never to hear in my life: "Oral, I'm taking you home to your parents."

When we got back to Ada, Papa helped the coach carry me in, and he sent for the doctors. Their verdict: tuberculosis.

The next few weeks and months became a bloody nightmare to me. Bloody, literally, because I almost hemorrhaged to death several times. A nightmare because I didn't have control anymore. And if I didn't have control . . . and God didn't have control . . . then my life was out of control completely.

I hated what was happening to me. I had been pulled back to the zero mark, and I was still losing ground. I was bitter. I was dying. And it didn't seem to me that there was anything I could do about it. I didn't understand that God could have a hand in my life if I would only let Him.

I was bedfast for five months, and during that time I lost forty-three pounds. I faced the possibility—really the *probability*—that I might never put my clothes and shoes back on again and go out to face life.

Is that where you are today? In your finances? In your relationships? In your health? Are you at rock bottom, your life and your dreams shattered?

Once I was flat on my back, people kept coming to the house to tell me about God. But they painted such a picture of God for me that I pretty much decided I didn't care to know Him. They'd say things that made me think, *God put this disease on me. He has my number.*

Even the pastor had this attitude. It seemed to me that he had only two songs. God was interested only in my soul, and I'd better get right with God so that I'd go to heaven when I died. The other song had only one verse: "Son, be patient."

Now when you're dying a lot faster than you're living, and especially when you're only seventeen, it's pretty hard to be patient.

Finally, Papa came to me and said, "Oral, you've got to get saved and give your life to God."

I didn't say anything.

He went on, "Son, don't you know how sick you are? Don't you realize that the doctors have signed the papers to send you to the sanatorium?" (In those days nearly all the people who went to the sanatorium never returned.)

Papa said, "As your father, as a Christian, as a minister of the Gospel, I've got to see you saved and know that you're going to heaven when you die." The way he said "when" sounded as if it could be any day or night.

I blurted out, "Papa, I don't want to go to heaven."

"What do you mean, you don't want to go to heaven?"

I said, "I want to *live*. I want to see some of my dreams realized. Papa, if God is half as good as you and Mama say He is, I've got a right to get well and to live. I don't want to go to heaven now."

I don't know if I should have said all that . . . but I did. And I'm glad I did, because it was a big part of my healing process. A slow boil started inside me that there was something wrong when we think God is mixed up in the diseases that come on our bodies. Or that God wants us to be patient when we get sick. That's against every medical precept I've ever known. It's certainly against what we teach at the Oral Roberts University School of Medicine and the City of Faith Health-Care Center.

When something goes bad that can possibly be corrected, don't get patient about it! *Jump* to make things start to happen to correct the situation.

I got mad.

And then I started looking for some good hard evidence about the way God really is.

My grandfather, Amos Pleasant Roberts, was a judge when Oklahoma was Indian Territory. He had a reputation for demanding that cases be based on good solid evidence. He didn't render judgments by whim or influence or circumstances around him. If he didn't have the evidence, he put off the trial until he got it.

Remembering him, I began to sift through all those things I had been hearing while I was lying there on that sickbed.

Strangely enough, I believed my family. They were evidence

to me. They were people I could see, feel, touch, hear. I had never seen God, and as far as I knew, I had never felt Him. But out where I grew up, folks made contracts with the spoken word. Their *word* was something you could count on. It was easier for me to take the word of my family as evidence than to believe anybody or anything else.

One day when my bedroom was full of kinfolks and neighbors, most of them carrying on about how God had made me sick, my mother rose up out of her chair and said with blazing eyes, "Now I'm not going to put up with this any longer."

The room got really quiet.

She said, "I've seen people get well when there wasn't any medical hope for them. I've seen God miraculously heal people, even through my own prayers when all other hope was gone. I've never believed that God goes around this earth picking out people to make them sick and die before their time."

And then she really let them have it.

She said, "Now you people start getting your thinking straight about God, or you can leave my home and stay away until you can come and *encourage* my son Oral."

And then she said one last thing I've never forgotten: "Whether my son lives or dies through this tuberculosis, I know that God is better than you are making Him out to be."

I took what Mama said as evidence: God is a good God.

Then I took what Papa began to *do* as evidence. Each night he would come and kneel at the foot of my bed and pray for me. Mama and the nurse joined him.

I was accustomed to hearing my parents pray. They had prayed aloud all my life. I listened for a while, and then my mind drifted away. Then, one night, I heard Papa's voice, but I heard another voice deep inside me, too.

It was like "Oral, Oral, Oral."

I looked at Papa. His eyes were closed, and tears were running down his face and dripping onto the floor. As I looked, his face seemed to fade away, and in a moment there was the countenance of Jesus. A bright light seemed to envelop Papa's face, and I had all the evidence I needed. God—a *good* God—was reaching out to me with tremendous love. The words came rushing up inside me, "Jesus, Jesus, save me."

I felt the presence of Jesus Christ enter my feet and go up through my entire body. A joy filled me, and I felt as light as a feather. It was so exhilarating I felt I could do anything. I had a sudden rush of energy, and Mama and Papa and I danced around the room, crying and laughing at the same time.

When my energy subsided, Mama and Papa helped me back to bed. Nothing had changed in my outward life. I still was a weak, dying seventeen-year-old boy whose body was ravaged by tuberculosis. But inside, everything had changed. I knew God was good. I knew He was *my* Savior. I had dealt God into my life and into my circumstance.

A few days later Jewel, my sister, came to my bedside. She leaned down and took my hand in hers. Without a waver to her voice or a flicker of an eyelash, she said seven words that I can still hear today. She said, "Oral, God is going to heal you."

There was a quiet force in her voice. Something stirred deep within me. "Is He, Jewel?" I asked.

"Yes, He is, Oral. He is going to heal you."

I took that as evidence: God is a healing God. I believed it. I believed I had a relationship with God.

I believed God was going to do something good for Oral Roberts.

I had counted God into my problem.

What about you?

Friend . . .

You must, *must*, *MUST* come to a place where you can say from the bottom of your heart: I believe God. He's real. He's now.

I believe God is totally *good*. He's on my side. I believe God is going to do something good for *me*. He's in the middle of my problem with me, and He's at work on the problem.

The way you come to that believing . . . that knowing . . . may be different from the way I came to it. The way you feel God . . . the way you experience His presence . . . may be different from the way I did. But what's important is that you reach a place deep down inside yourself where you know that you know that you know that you *know*. It is important for you to be able to say, "God almighty is my partner in solving this problem, in overcoming this difficulty, in meeting this need, in bringing me out of this negative circumstance into greater wholeness. God is with *me* on my road to recovery."

Then get ready for something to start happening.

Several things started happening to me right away.

First, I started to see my doctors in a different light. I had three physicians, Dr. Craig, Dr. King, and Dr. Shi. I had not cooperated with them. In my hurt I had seen them almost as the enemy. They were involved in my sickness, and my sickness was bad; the association between them and badness had become solid. But suddenly I started to see that they were on my side.

Not one of them had said, "Son, be patient." All three of my doctors were trying with all the skill they had to get me well. They were on the side of health. In fact, I have yet to meet a doctor who is not positive for health. Instead of resisting their efforts, I started cooperating with them in a new way. We started encouraging one another.

I had just about given up on taking the medicine that these doctors prescribed. As I lay on my bed, with people telling me I was going to die and my attitude so low that I had to look up to see bottom, I had come to the place where I didn't see any point in doing what the doctors said. The medicine tasted awful, and I decided it just wasn't worth taking if I was going to die anyway. After I counted God into my problem, I began to see the medicine in a different way. It was made from chemicals that were in God's earth. God could *use* that medicine to help me. It might be part of His plan. I started taking my medicine regularly and following the doctors' directions.

A second thing happened. A man of God came to a little town about eighteen miles away from my home. He pitched a tent and started preaching that God had sent His Son Jesus to heal physically as well as to save spiritually.

My brother Elmer and his wife were living in that little community where the evangelist had set up his tent. My brother was not deeply religious or serious about his Christian life at that time. But his wife was. And Elmer went with her to this man's meetings. They saw him lay hands on people and pray for them. And some of them began to show evidence that they were healed or on the road to recovery.

Elmer was like the rest of us Robertses. He didn't believe everything he saw or heard. But he finally saw enough to take it as good evidence.

The next thing we knew, Elmer drove to our house, and he walked into my bedroom telling me, "Get up, Oral, and get dressed. I've come to take you to be prayed for."

I said, "Elmer, I can't. I'm too weak."

He said, "I'll dress you."

Mama and Papa came in and asked what was happening. When Elmer explained, Mama began to rejoice. She seemed to know that something good was going to happen. My father began to cry. They dressed me, and then Elmer picked me up, mattress and all, and put me on the backseat of the car he had borrowed. He had spent his last money before payday to buy enough gasoline for the trip.

As we rode along to that meeting—pain shooting through my body at every bump in the road—I listened to Elmer telling us what he had seen and heard at the meetings. It lodged in me. I started expecting something to happen.

Then Elmer's voice faded away, and I heard another voice deep inside me that grew louder until it seemed to fill my entire head and body with a roaring:

"Son, I'm going to heal you, and you're to take My healing power to your generation."

Nobody had to tell me that the voice was God's voice. Nobody will have to tell you when you hear Him. He may not speak to you in the same way. He may not say the same things. But you'll know that you know that you know that God is doing the talking.

And I made a conscious, definite, firm decision to obey God, even though I didn't fully understand what those words meant.

That *commitment to obey* was like a seal on a new attitude and a new direction in my life.

I had once been a fast-moving guy, hell-bent on doing my thing. Then I made a decision to believe God . . . to believe God is a good God . . . and to make God a part of my life. I started to look for ways that I might cooperate with God in the events and people and situations of my life. And that day in the backseat of the car on the way to an evangelistic meeting, I made a decision to *obey* God without apology and with all my being. Now that's what you might call a 180-degree turnaround.

There was one more important thing that happened.

Elmer drove the car up to where the tent was pitched. My parents took a rocking chair into the meeting, and then they carried me and put me in it, with pillows to my side and back. Mama and Papa sat on either side of me. There were about fourteen hundred people in the tent that day, which was a really big meeting for those times in that part of the country.

I didn't hear a lot of what the preacher was saying. I was feverish, and my lungs hurt. At times I felt like I was being cut straight through with a knife until the pain came out underneath my shoulder blades.

As the man of God preached and then began to pray for others—about two hours or more—another kind of voice began to whisper inside me. I had heard it before, but I never tried to identify it or think it was bad or shut it up.

The message was something like this: "Now aren't you something? You could be home in bed with some peace and quiet. Instead you're over here in this tent with a bunch of crazy people who are thinking that God heals. You really think *you're* going to be healed? Just because your sister said it? Just because your brother came over and got you out of bed? Boy, are you ever sick. You've got tuberculosis. You're going to the sanatorium any day now. You aren't ever going to come out of there. You're going to die."

I could have done one of two things when those thoughts started distracting me and filling my being. I could have listened to them. But I chose the other approach: I got mad. I just flat out refused to listen. I got stubborn, and I refused to accept the lying, negative whispers.

God is *never* negative. That's one thing about which I'm absolutely convinced. God has never been negative—not one time, not in any situation, *never*.

You say, "Oral Roberts, you're pretty sure about that."

Absolutely sure.

God doesn't even know how to think a negative thought. He has absolutely never had a negative attitude. There is no way that He would, could, or might cause a bad, discouraging, depressing attitude to dwell in you.

God is a *good* God, and *He will always be a good God*.

Now let's get this right down to where you are. I believe God has something better in store for you than what you've got right now. Even if your situation in life is pretty good, God wants something *better* for you. He wants greater health, a better marriage or personal relationships, stronger family ties, increased prosperity, higher self-esteem and feelings of self-worth.

You have some choices to make about what *you* want. Do you want a better situation for yourself?

If you do, count God in.

Make the choice to believe: God is real.

Make the choice to believe: God is on my side. He's involved in my life and in my circumstances.

Make the choice to believe: God is involved and concerned about *this particular specific need* that I have, whatever it may be. Name it. Identify it. And then say, "God is concerned about my sickness, my health, my finances, my marriage, my family, my relationships, my feelings, my hurt, my pain, my *life*."

Make the choice to obey God in whatever ways He may direct you.

And finally, make the choice to shut your mind to the negative lies that come against you once you've decided to obey God and follow His leading in your life.

What happens if you do *not* make these choices?

I don't know of any guarantees for you. From my experience, I'd have to predict failure, delay, confusion, detours, discouragement, pain.

What happens when you *do* make these choices?

You're on the road to recovery, facing the right direction. I'm as certain of that as I am of my name!

What happened to me that evening as I sat in my rocking chair, hearing a man of God preach and then pray for the sick?

Well, I was the last person to be prayed for. Mama and Papa stood me up so he could pray for me.

I heard a prayer like I had never heard before. And I was ready to hear it. That's a powerful combination. When you hear the right words and you're ready to hear them, things can really happen.

This man came toward me and said a prayer that went something like this:

"You foul tormenting disease. I command you in the Name of Jesus Christ of Nazareth to loose this boy's life and lungs. Loose him, and let him go free!"

I had never heard a prayer so definite or more to the point in my entire life. I certainly knew this wasn't a namby-pamby, milk-toast, God-help-Oral-to-be-patient prayer. I knew intuitively that this was the kind of prayer that was more apt to cause healing to burst forth in my life! I knew I was in the right place at the right time for something *good* to happen to me.

The words of that man whipped through me like a lashing wind. And I received them. I didn't mentally fight against them. I didn't stand there full of cynicism. I wasn't dwelling on what-if or why-not thoughts. I let that prayer become a part of my life.

A warmth started flooding up inside me. It didn't start in my lungs first. I felt it start in my feet, come up through my legs and body, and engulf my entire being. The next thing I knew, my lungs began to feel like lungs again.

You know, before I had tuberculosis, I didn't really think much about having lungs. They just worked, and that's the way it was.

When I got sick, I became aware of my lungs with every

breath I took. And as I stood there receiving healing prayer into my life, my lungs felt as if strong, soft hands were settling them down, putting them back into good working order. The sharp, shooting pains were leaving.

I'd grown up a stutterer. In many ways I had lived inside myself because I couldn't talk like others. If you had asked my family before that night, "Will Oral be able to say anything about it if he's healed?" they probably would have said no.

But God is a God of *wholeness*.

When God heals us, He begins a process to put us back together so that our attitudes and our bodies are one working unit. The same power that had welled up inside me and engulfed my lungs had also loosened my tongue.

When the evangelist said, "Son, do you have anything to say?" I found that I had a *lot* to say. It was like a dam breaking and the water rushing forth.

Friend . . . I had experienced the healing power of God. Yes, I had a *lot* to say.

When you count God in on your problem and you get committed to doing things in your life *His* way, then His healing power will begin to affect every area of your life. God is a God of wholeness. You may think it's a financial problem, but when your faith and God's power begin to move against that financial need, you're going to find that the miracle will affect every area of your life—your health, your relationships, your attitudes and feelings about yourself.

You may think you have a problem with a spouse, but when your faith and God's power begin to move against that problem and restore the relationship, you're going to find a lot of other things starting to be different, too.

Your "recovery" is not going to be in just one area. It's going to start a recovery . . . a regaining . . . a restoring of your entire life.

Get ready for what I have to say to you next. It's the first signpost you're going to face as you move toward the full recovery that God has for you. . . .

Consider

1. What do you dream of being and doing in your life?

2. Is there something that keeps you from doing what God is calling you to do? Is rebellion against God standing in the way of your receiving your miracle?

3. Have you made a *commitment* in your life to obey God—no matter the circumstances?

4. When you really stop to think about it, do you (by your words and actions) *discourage* or *encourage* those around you to believe for God's best in their lives?

Decide Specifically What You're Believing For

Bob DeWeese—how I have loved him as my Christian brother, my associate evangelist, my colleague since 1951, and now the chairman of our board of regents at Oral Roberts University.

Bob is a man of great encouragement and faith. Except in one area of his life. Since his father died with a heart attack at age sixty-seven, Bob got it into his head that he would never live past his father's age.

"But, Bob," I protested years ago, "your mother is in her seventies and healthy."

Years went by, and I said, "She's in her eighties, Bob, and in good health."

Still later, "Your mother is ninety and still going strong."

Bob's response to me always was, "I know, I know. But I'm taking after Dad, not Mother. I'll die at sixty-seven or before."

"Bob, you are stronger than I am and than most people I know. You were an Olympic swimmer. You are still a good athlete in your forties." And later "in your fifties" and then "in your sixties."

Bob would just laugh and say, "Oral, I'm a Dutchman from Kansas. I have a hard head, and this is just the way I think."

"But, Bob, you're a Christian before you're a Dutchman or a Kansan. We're in healing evangelism. We're trying to follow God's system, not merely man's. We're trying to use our faith so something *good* will continually be coming into our lives."

Bob could agree with that for everyone else in the world . . . but not for himself.

Then one day several years ago I got a call to come quickly to the hospital. Bob, at sixty-seven, was down with a heart attack. He had a second attack in the hospital, and only the hard-working and alert doctors, with their great machines and fine facilities, were able to keep his body functioning. Bob actually saw the edges of heaven and started to enter it . . . when someone called him back.

I went to the hospital, and Charlotte, Bob's wife, got permission from the doctor for me to see Bob. He was happy as a lark. He had worked with me through the years in the great crusades, had been a pastor, and had done good work for the Lord, and now he was *eager* to go to heaven. He was *happy* at the thought of getting there as soon as possible.

I prayed for Bob and with Bob, but I didn't feel a release in my spirit. I wasn't depressed about Bob's homegoing. But something tugged deep in my heart that maybe God wanted Bob to do something here on the earth that hadn't been done yet.

As I thanked the doctors and nurses and prepared to leave the hospital, I saw Bob's teenaged granddaughter sitting in the waiting room outside the intensive care unit. She had grown up in our crusades, often sitting with her mother or grandmother on the front row of the big tent or in auditoriums, hearing her granddad preach and hearing me preach and seeing me pray for the sick.

As I passed by her she said, "Oral Roberts, you didn't pray a tent prayer for my granddad!"

I said, "Well, this is not my hospital or where I'm in charge. I did the best I could. Besides, your granddad's mind is made up."

She said very frankly as the tears rolled, "I sat in the big tents as a little girl. I heard you pray. I saw God heal people. And you're not doing it today for my granddad like you did then for those people."

What miracle
do you need
today?

Ask God for it
specifically.

She started to cry, and between her sobs she said, "Please go back in there and really *pray* for my granddad!"

The Holy Spirit moved in me, and I turned and asked the doctors if I could see Bob again.

When Bob saw me, he said, "Did you forget something?"

"Almost."

"What?"

"My tent prayer."

He looked puzzled. I said, "I didn't pray for you like I used to pray for people who came through the healing line in our tent crusades."

He smiled. "That was something, wasn't it?"

"Bob," I said, "your granddaughter is upset. She remembers. She remembers how God worked through you and me. She remembers the anointing that broke the yoke of sickness, sin, fear, poverty, and everything else that was not of God in those people's lives."

He seemed genuinely puzzled until I said, "How old was your dad when he died?"

"You know, Oral, he was sixty-seven. You aren't thinking of that, are you?"

"Yes. I am thinking of that. How old are you now?"

"Sixty-seven."

"How old was your mother when she went to heaven recently?"

"Ninety-two."

"Ninety-two?"

"Yes."

"And you chose your dad's genes over hers?"

"Now, Oral."

"Okay. Let me ask you some questions. If you're happy with the answers, I'll get out of here and let you go."

I had his attention now. "Ask me," he said.

"In your heart of hearts, are you finished with what God has called you to do?"

"I think so."

"Are you sure?"

No answer.

"Bob, in all these years I've known you, you've talked about being like your father and dying when you were sixty-seven. Directly or indirectly, have you chosen your father's experience? Have you been holding on to a wrong attitude?"

"Maybe. I'm not sure."

"Do you trust me, Bob?"

"With all my heart."

"Okay. Then I'm going to level with you like I see it. It may be that sixty-seven is your year of appointment to die. It may be that your genes and your father's are alike. Or it may be that God isn't through with you and you can change your attitude and decide to believe for something else."

Bob looked at me sharply. "Like what?"

"Like decide to believe for your *mother's* genes."

We were both in uncharted territory. The medical people were doing their job as it seemed best to them. I was doing my job, too.

"If you are willing, I will pray again, Bob. But not like before. I'm not a doctor, and I don't know anything scientific about genes. But I'll have to pray exactly how I feel it inside me. At least I can face your granddaughter then. And God can do what He pleases."

"Well," he said slowly, "I guess we have nothing to lose."

"That's not good enough, Bob," I said. "It's yes or no. It's go or it's no go. You know, and I know, there are times when a man of God speaks or prays and it's like Jesus speaking again on the earth. Things happen!"

"How well I know," he said. And then he added with a greater firmness in his voice, "Go ahead."

My prayers are for the most part brief and to the point. Often they are only one or two words. I heard myself saying, "Bob, do you choose your father's genes or your mother's genes?"

Faintly, he said, "Mother's."

"Say it so I can hear you!"

"Mother's!" And then he began to laugh that big infectious laugh of his. "But, Oral, I've already been to heaven. I'm not sure I don't want to go back there."

"Okay, I'm gone."

"No, wait!"

"Listen, Bob," I said, "I'm not going to impose anything on you, certainly not my own desires. It's your life."

"You're serious, aren't you?"

"Yes," I said. "Very serious."

"Pray," he said.

And I prayed, "Jesus, Bob DeWeese has chosen his mother's genes. He wants to live beyond that hang-up he's had for years about his father's death. I ask You, grant it in Jesus' name! Amen and amen."

I turned to leave, and Bob's body began to shake until he nearly fell out of the bed. Charlotte, who had slipped into the room along with a couple of nurses, helped me roll his six-foot-three-inch body back onto the bed. Again, his body shook. It was not a normal shaking. It was a shaking under the Spirit of God. The entire room seemed to fill up with light, and I could feel enough heavenly power, I thought, to heal hundreds or even thousands.

When I left, Bob was cheerful. I left quietly and calmly. As I passed Cindy, she smiled. "He'll live. Don't worry. Those tent prayers still work."

"Cindy," I said, "it wasn't a tent prayer. You remember prayers that were positives, prayers that expected results from a good God? Sometimes it's a matter of deciding what you're going to pray *for* and what you're going to believe *for*."

Bob DeWeese is alive and healthy as a horse at this writing nearly seven years later.

Now I'm not going to promise you or anybody else that what happened to Bob DeWeese is going to happen for you. Bob will tell you that God healed him when he made the change in his attitude and started to believe for something different in his life. What I *can* say to you with certainty is this: God has put it in your control to *decide what you are going to believe for.*

How much health do you want to have?

Specifically.

You may say, "Well, I just want to be healthy."

How healthy? There are different degrees of being healthy. Do you just want to be free of a particular disease or pain in your body? Or do you want to really have fine health? Are you willing to lose the extra pounds and exercise in the right ways to have the greatest amount of health you can possibly have? Are you willing to quit smoking or give up other bad health habits in order to get God's best health for you?

How much health do you want to have?

How good do you want your marriage to be? Specifically.

How much prosperity do you want to have? Specifically.

Name the problem in your life, and then name its solution. The *best* solution. How good a solution are you believing for?

When I was in my late twenties, I was the pastor of a church . . . a husband . . . a father of two small children . . . and a student continuing my education at the university. It seemed I was always in a hurry and not getting anywhere very fast. Do you know that feeling?

Each morning I had a habit of reading a little in the Bible before I ran out to catch the bus that would take me to the university.

One morning as I ran out to catch the bus, I realized that I had forgotten to read the Bible, so I ran back in and grabbed my Bible. It fell open to the little book of 3 John in the New Testament. I started reading, and the second verse of that book leaped out at me as if it was the first time I'd ever seen it.

Now I had read the New Testament through more than one hundred times and had never noticed that particular verse. "Evelyn," I shouted. "Did you know this was in the Bible?" And then I read the verse to her: "Beloved, I pray that you may prosper in all things and be in health, just as your soul prospers" (3 John 2).

Evelyn looked at me and said, "Oral, is that in the Bible?"

I said, "It sure is. It's right here."

And she said, "Well, why didn't you find it before, if you've read the New Testament so many times?"

I said, "I don't know."

And then she asked me, "Do you believe it?"

I said, "Of course I believe it. It's in the Bible."

We were so low in our finances that if we had died, they would have had to jack us up to bury us. All the furniture in our entire house didn't cost three hundred dollars. I'd put my elbows on the dining room table, and the thing would fall over in my lap.

You see, Evelyn and I had both been taught that Christians should be poor. We regularly gave the tithe—a tenth of our money—to the church, but we were never taught to expect anything back from God. We gave our money because we were supposed to and that was that; it was gone. We'd never learned to receive back from God or to enjoy His blessings in our lives. This caused a serious shortfall in our finances.

Something happened to both Evelyn and me the day we read that verse. It was an exciting time that morning. I didn't go to the university that day. Instead, we sat down and pored over our Bibles trying to find other things God said that might give us more information about how to receive from God and about how God wants to bless His people with health and all-around prosperity. We talked and cried and laughed and praised the Lord.

And then I said, "Evelyn, what we're discovering in the Word of God means that we're *supposed* to prosper as God's people. The Lord wants us to. Do you believe that if I asked the Lord for a new car, He would give us one?"

Evelyn said, "No, Oral, I really don't."

One thing about Evelyn—she's always honest. I was determined, though, to see if God meant what He said. "Well, then I'll believe for a new car by myself," I said. And I meant it.

We were driving an old nineteen-hundred-and-something Chevrolet in those days. One day, shortly before the morning we discovered 3 John 2 in the Bible, I had backed out of our driveway and hit my neighbor's car. I put a big dent in it. My first thought was, *Oh, well, he'll never know I did it*. And then I thought, *But I'll know. I'll know*. So I parked my car and got out and knocked on his door, and this big man came to the door and said, "Yes?"

I said, "Mister, I just ran into your car."

"You did?"

I said, "Yes, and if you will have an estimate made, I will pay for the damages."

He seemed a little embarrassed and said, "Oh, go on, go on."

I said, "No. I mean it. I'll do it."

He said, "Go on, go on." And we left it at that. I waited to hear from him.

Now a few days *after* Evelyn and I had read 3 John 2 together, I was out mowing my lawn, and this neighbor leaned over the fence and said, "Hey there, young man. I've been noticing that old car of yours. You need a *new* car, don't you?"

"That's an understatement," I said.

"How would you like to have a new car?"

I said, "I'd like it."

"Well," he said, "I'll tell you what to do. I'm a car dealer."

"You are?" I didn't know that.

He said, "You bring your car down, and I'll sell it at the highest price. Then I will let you have a brand-new car at my cost."

And do you know, he was a Buick dealer.

In those days the Buick was the ultimate car for people like us. Everybody we knew hoped someday to be able to drive a Buick.

Well, it happened just as that man said. He sold our car high, and then he sent us to the factory so we could buy a Buick at his cost and drive it back to Oklahoma. The difference was just a few hundred dollars.

On the way back home Evelyn said, "Stop the car, Oral. Stop the car."

"What's wrong?" I asked.

She said, "This is really the answer to 3 John 2 you read to me. The Lord said He wanted us to prosper. This is the first step. And now I know that He really *will* supply our needs in this life."

We got out and dedicated that car to the Lord and had prayer together. Something important happened to us that day.

We began to believe that God wanted us to have more in this life than we wanted. God *wanted* to meet our needs and to meet them with *abundance*. Another verse in the Bible came alive for us: "The thief [the devil] does not come except to steal, and to kill, and to destroy. I have come that they may have life, and that they may have it more *abundantly*" (John 10:10, italics added).

Evelyn and I came to realize that God didn't want us to just barely make it through this life . . . to eke out a bare existence . . . to be always on the brink of want . . . to barely cope with life. No. God wanted us to be on top of life. He wanted us to have *all* our needs met. He wanted us to have a *great* marriage, not just a good marriage. He wanted us to have *great* joy, not just a little happiness now and then. He wanted us to be in *good* health, not just "pretty good" health.

That Buick was far more than a new car to us. It was one of the most important lessons we've ever learned in our lives. It was proof that God is a God of blessing and that when we are in partnership with God in this life, we can strive for the best God has for us and expect to receive it.

You might say, "Well, what should I ask for specifically?"

What's the best you can imagine and believe for?

I'm not saying that lightly. I'm very serious. What can you conceive and believe for?

One day in the early 1950s I was driving down a highway in the great Pacific Northwest. I was facing a staggering problem. It was good for me to have some time alone to think and meditate and give the Lord time to speak to my heart.

The beautiful Columbia River flowed to my left for several hundred miles, and the countryside was alive with color and the autumn harvests.

I've never been a person who can live with a need. Something has to give—me or the need.

A big need was challenging me that day. I felt small and inadequate. In contrast to that, I saw the farmers of that fertile valley reaping their harvests. Trucks loaded with wheat would pass me on the highway. Occasionally a deer would run out from the thick brush and cross in front of me.

Then as I passed through the area where the famous Delicious apples are raised, I saw refrigerated railcars being loaded to carry them to markets throughout America. Everywhere I looked, nature was in production. Seed had been planted, the soil cultivated, the mighty reproductive forces had produced the harvest, and the people were excited and happy. It was one of the most inspiring sights I had ever experienced.

As I meditated on this, a thought came crystal clear: *Whatever you can conceive and believe, you can do!*

It was God speaking in my heart from the teaching in the Bible about His creative power. It was a reminder of the way He created the earth, made man, and instituted the laws of *sowing and reaping*. It was a reminder that He had sent His Son, Jesus Christ, to earth to give man abundant life. All at once I saw that God's purpose was carried on through *faith*, not only in the beginning, not only when Jesus was on earth, but in the *now*.

I could feel my inner man begin to stir. I could feel myself standing up on the inside. I became excited as I began to believe the very thought that had been conceived in my mind:

"Whatever you can conceive and believe, you can do!"

I began to understand how God had first conceived the world and man. I saw He had *believed*. God had believed in man enough to create him with the power to choose good or evil, to live positively or negatively, to believe or to doubt, to respond to God or to denounce Him. God believed so much in man that even when man went his own way and sinned, bringing suffering and death into the world, God sent His only begotten Son as the seed of His faith to bring man back to the place where he could be redeemed, receive a new life, and have life abundantly.

I saw clearly how faith, when planted as a seed and rightly tended, is the key to everything.

I saw clearly that God believed in me and wanted my good *far more* than even I believed in myself and wanted my own good. Put another way, I couldn't outbelieve God. I couldn't outconceive God. *Anything* that I conceived and believed for, I could one day receive.

You may say, "Well, Oral Roberts, how much is *too* much?"

I don't know. I've never met anybody who had the ability to conceive and believe for too much of God's goodness in life. The problem is usually in the other direction. People think thoughts that are *too little*. People believe *too little*. People expect *too little* from God. People have planted too few seeds of their faith. And then they use lots of excuses to explain why they are unable to conceive and believe for more.

Frankly, I've never met a person—or known of a person—who received too much from God. Now I've known some people who *hoarded* too much of what they received. They haven't been free to stay in the rhythm of "giving and receiving" with what they get of God's blessings. It's like a water pipe that gets clogged in their lives. Things start to stagnate, and pretty soon they aren't much good to themselves or to others or to God's work in this world. *But that isn't a problem of receiving from God. That's a problem of hoarding and clinging to what is received.*

Jesus faced that very issue head-on. He told a story about a rich man who really prospered. And the man began to say, "What shall I do with all this wealth? I don't have enough room to store it. I'll tear down my barns and build greater barns, and I'll put all of my additional goods there. Then I'll say to my soul: 'Soul, you have enough to last you for many years, and now you can just take it easy—eat, drink, and be merry.'"

And God said, "That's not the way it will be. The great wealth you have gathered up isn't really yours. Your soul is going to be required, you're going to die tonight, and then what will happen to all of this wealth?" (See Luke 12:16–21.)

God wasn't saying that it was wrong for this man to be prosperous . . . for him to succeed . . . for him to get the wealth he had. After all, he had planted the seeds for his harvests. No. What was wrong was his attitude about what he should do with it after he got it. And with this wrong attitude, what did he do?

First, he ignored his spiritual man, and fed himself with only material things. He blotted out of his mind the impossibility of being happy while neglecting a proper balance between spiritual and material values.

Second, he tried to hoard what he had. He was reluctant to multiply his life by investing a portion of it for God's purposes or to help others or to build something for the kingdom of God.

Third, he started to trust in his wealth and make it his source of happiness, instead of trusting in God who is the only true Source to fulfill his life.

And those are the three places where people become confused in their thinking about money. It's true about every aspect of life and not only about money.

Earn as much as you can . . . so you can give as much as you can. Get as much wealth as you can . . . so you can bless and inspire others, honor the Lord, and really turn the economics of this world around so it enlarges your life *and* the kingdom of God on earth.

Be in as good health as you can be . . . so you have the energy to do more and give more to others and do the work that the Lord puts in front of you.

Have the best marriage you can possibly have . . . so you can share your life in an overflowing way with others and raise happy children to bless this earth and carry on God's plan.

Have the best friendships you can have . . . so together you and your friends can multiply the talents and time and love you have and bless this world in Jesus' name.

Don't settle for this world's dregs when you can have God's best!

So let me ask you again, What *specifically* are you believing for in your life? What do you *want* God to do?

You know, Jesus stopped one day as He was walking on the road out of Jericho. He stopped because a blind man called out to Him. Now Jesus could see that this man was blind. He was dressed like a blind man. He was begging by the side of the road like the blind people did. He looked blind. But Jesus asked him, "What do you want?" In other words, "What do you want *Me* to do for *you?*"

It was only after the blind man said, "I want to see," that Jesus healed him and he received his eyesight. (See Mark 10:46–52.)

It's very important that you decide what you want from God . . . what you're willing to believe for . . . what your miracle looks like, feels like, acts like, is like.

On your road to recovery, how are you going to know when you arrive? That's the point. Decide today. You may need to face several issues as you decide. Let's deal with them right now. . . .

Consider

1. What are *you* believing for today? Name the solution you want for your problem. How *good* is the solution you want? Are you believing for God's *best*? What is the best you can imagine and believe for?

2. What is the difference in your life between the cycle of giving-receiving-giving-receiving and giving-receiving-hoarding?

3. Are you trusting in something or someone other than God for the miracle you need? Are you trusting your spouse? Your bank account? Your employer?

4. What is the difference between God as your SOURCE and people as your source?

Trade in Your Poor Attitudes and Poor Dreams for Exciting New Ones

I have laughingly said to many audiences, "The best thing I ever did in life was to choose my parents." Of course you know I didn't choose my parents. The point I'm making is that I got specially blessed by our good God who saw to it that I was born a son of the Ellis Melvin and Claudius Priscilla Roberts family.

Papa went to heaven at age eighty-seven, Mama at eighty-nine. My brothers, Elmer and Vaden, are still alive and so is my sister, Jewel. They are very dear to me. They are dear beyond the fact that they are my blood relatives. They helped me choose much of the good attitude I have today. They taught me a good attitude.

That's a key point for you to understand. Where did you get your attitude? You learned it. Somebody taught you an attitude, and you bought it. Or somebody tried to teach you, and you didn't buy it. You weren't born with an attitude or dreams about what your life might one day be. You may have been inclined toward it, but you *learned* your attitude. Your dreams grew out of that attitude.

A second key point here is closely related: You can *unlearn* an attitude if you choose to. You don't have to think the way you always have thought. Your attitude hasn't been set in concrete somewhere.

Let me emphasize that point: *You* can unlearn your attitude, but you have to want to. Nobody else can do it for you. New attitudes can result in new dreams. Nobody else can dream your dreams.

Nobody else can dream Oral Roberts's dreams. I must dream them because nobody else can have my exact attitude but me. Nobody else has the exact learning experiences in life that gave rise to that attitude; therefore I must take charge of my attitude.

I was born into a healthy family—the fifth and last child. My oldest sister, Velma, was a beautiful baby. As a little girl she could sing almost like a nightingale. Her mind was bright, and her body was sturdy. When she was just getting old enough to go to school, something went wrong. Nobody really knows what. Mama and Papa have told me that over a period of weeks she became an epileptic, and she continued to get worse until her mind was affected. But she died at nineteen, not from epilepsy but from pneumonia.

I was only about three years old when Velma died, and I don't remember much about her. But years later when I became ill with tuberculosis, there were folks who remembered Velma, and their thinking ran something like this:

"When one of those Robertses gets something in their lungs, it's the end. Velma died. Now Oral's going fast."

That attitude wasn't without a grain or two of truth. Velma *had* died. Mama's people were Indian, and the number one disease of the Indians then and now was lung disease. Mama's father and her two older sisters had died of a lung disease. Mama's Indian relatives were not talkative people, but they had passed the signal that I with my Indian blood would die with the Indian's disease. That belief was a form of superstition, and I remember it to this day.

The main thing about that kind of attitude is that it is a *deadly* one. It did absolutely nothing to help me or anyone else get well and stay well. Instead it embedded itself in my mind and became a serious hindrance to my having faith that I could have a chance to recover.

Maybe you have an attitude that goes something like this:

*God isn't limited
to your limitations.
He has methods
beyond your knowledge.
He has blessings
beyond your desires.
God has more for you
than you are taking
advantage of.*

*Make a commitment today to learn
to do things the way God does them . . .
to think as God thinks . . .
to speak as God speaks.*

"Well, arthritis [or any other disease you want to name] runs in my family. My mother had it, and my grandmother had it, so I guess I'm going to get it, too."

or

"A lot of people in our area seem to be getting cancer. I'll probably get it, too, sometime."

or

"Folks are going out of business right and left in this region. The economy is falling apart. I'll probably lose my job (or my business), too."

or

"Just about every other marriage seems to end in divorce these days. Guess mine will eventually."

or

"Things are really getting tough everywhere. I dread the bad things that are going to happen to me."

If you have an attitude like one of these, it is no more than superstition.

Stop it. Change it. Get rid of it. It will do absolutely *nothing* to help your health or start a recovery process in you. Like attracts like.

Let me tell you what that wrong type of thinking does to you. It puts a blindfold over your ability to conceive and believe. That type of thinking literally keeps you from being able to conceive of what God's best might be for your life or from being able to believe that it's possible for you to have what God wants you to have.

If you think you're about to go under . . . how can you believe for going over the top?

If you think you're going to fail . . . how can you believe God that you'll be able to win?

If you think you're about to die . . . how can you live successfully?

There's another set of attitudes that can destroy you. They go something like this:

"Well, my daddy earned this much money and had this

kind of house. Now I earn even a little more and have a little bit better house. That's it. I've arrived."

or

"We've been doing things this way in the company for the last twenty years. Guess that's just the best we can do."

or

"I got C's all through high school. Guess I'll get C's in college."

or

"I failed at that, so I'm not going to risk failing a second time."

Friend, remember that like attracts like. That type of thinking will not attract God's blessings to you but will blind you to seeing that God's best should be yours.

There's an old story about a man who died and went to heaven. When he got there, one of God's angels was giving him a guided tour of heaven. They passed many beautiful buildings, but finally they came to one that was bigger than all the others. The man stopped the angel and said, "What's in that huge building?" And the angel said sadly, "That building is filled with all of the things that God would have liked for you to have had on earth, but you didn't ask Him for them or believe He'd give them to you."

Are you aware that your past mistakes don't dictate your future success unless you allow them to?

It's your faith—your ability to conceive and believe—that will dictate your future success. It's your attitude that will give rise to your dreams. If you've got a negative, defeated, sick, down attitude, you're going to have weak, shallow, small dreams.

What about this type of talk?

"Did you hear that she has cancer. Isn't it just awful? I wonder how long she has to live?"

or

"Heart attack. You know, he'll never get over it. Poor guy."

Stop it!

If I could say it to you a million times, until it filled every cell in your being, stop it, stop it, *stop it!*

Don't let those attitudes take root in you. If you hear someone voice those attitudes, don't listen. Don't spread it to others. That type of thinking can pull you down and slow you up until you'll be flat on your back, paralyzed in your spirit.

And while I'm at it, I'm going to share another deadly attitude that affected my life in those early days of my youth. Now this wasn't an attitude that my family had at all. But a lot of people I knew had the notion:

"If you believe God can heal miraculously, you don't need a doctor."

I don't know where they learned that attitude. I just know it was emphasized in my childhood. The Bible says, "The prayer of faith will save the sick" (James 5:15). It also says, "Those who are sick need a physician." That's in Luke 5:31. Jesus Himself said it, and that settles it for me.

I believe—and I've always preached it, too—that doctors are used by God. Medicines are used by God. Prayer is used by God. Sometimes a different diet or exercise program or climate is used by God to help a person. These are all God's methods, and He uses them all for your benefit.

If you think you don't need a doctor . . .

If you think you shouldn't take the medicines you need (which are chemicals from the Lord's earth that He made and put there for our use) . . .

If you think you don't need to follow the advice that a competent physician gives you . . .

Then in my experience and best judgment you need to change your attitude. Get a better one. Start believing: *God has put all these things here for my health. God wants me well. He uses many methods. I'm going to open myself up to them. I'm going to get the best health I can have.*

I've also met some folk who don't believe in the power of prayer. They shut it out of their minds and lives. I did that once, to my detriment. If you have a negative attitude about the power of God to work through prayer . . . change your attitude.

"Well," you say, "I've never seen anyone who was healed through prayer."

Take it from me. I have. I've seen thousands upon thousands of people whom God dealt with directly and decisively through the power of prayer—both my prayers and the prayers of others. God heals through prayer. It's one of His methods. Don't limit yourself by a closed attitude.

Let me put it this way:

God has power beyond your limits.

God has methods beyond your knowledge.

God has blessings beyond your desires.

God has more for you than you are taking advantage of.

And you'll never get all God has for you if you continue to hang on to poor attitudes and poor dreams.

Take stock today. What is the best you hope for? Why is your thinking so narrow . . . or shortsighted . . . or limited?

What happens if you have dreamed big and failed? Let's deal with that next so you can get over that hurdle and on down the road of recovery to *wholeness*. . . .

Consider

1. Where did you learn most of the attitudes *you* have? Are they good attitudes? Are they godly attitudes?

2. Are you expecting bad to come into your life? Why? Do you know where you learned that attitude?

3. Have you decided how God *won't* heal you, the methods you are sure He *won't* use? Why? Do you know where you learned those attitudes?

4. Have you put a ceiling on what you can hope for in life? Why? Do you know where you learned those attitudes?

Make a Better Vow

Have you ever made a vow in your life?

Many mothers and fathers make vows to raise their children in the ways of the Lord. Husbands and wives make vows to love each other through thick and thin.

Many have broken those vows.

The fact is that every human being alive makes vows in some form or another. Some have said to God, "If You'll save me from this car wreck, I'll live for You." Or, "If You'll just heal this person I love, I'll quit sinning."

And many have forgotten those vows.

Maybe you find yourself in that position today. The marriage vow has been broken. The promise to God has been shattered. If that is the case, I've got some encouraging words for you today.

First, don't try to deny that vows shape your life. Don't put your pledge to God aside and try to convince yourself that it didn't matter. Vows are serious business.

Three months before my mother gave birth to me, she was on her way to pray for a neighbor's sick child. A storm was brewing—a powerful, typical Oklahoma thunderstorm—and the winds were so fierce they nearly kept her from moving forward. As my little five-foot Indian mother pushed her way against this wind to get to the neighbor's house, she made a vow to God: "O God, I ask You to heal my neighbor's child tonight, and when mine is born, I'll give him to You to preach the Gospel."

The child had double pneumonia in a time when there was no cure for it. But the Lord healed him miraculously, and Mama often told me when I was a little boy about how she had given me to God with her vow. All my life she expected that someday I would preach the Gospel and serve the Lord. And when I consider it now, I find it no mere coincidence that her promise about my life was made in relation to a child who was dying of a lung disease and that I was later healed of an incurable lung disease.

As a young stuttering child, I would often say to Mama, "How can I ever preach the Gospel? I can't even talk." And she would say, "Son, God will loose your tongue and enable you to preach. I made a vow to Him."

Through the years as my ministry grew and reached around the world to touch all the continents and scores of nations, I often thought of Mama's vow.

I made a vow when I began this ministry that I'd never touch the gold or the glory. A man said to me once, "Oral, they all say that you have a lot of money and that you're even a multimillionaire. As long as they all think it, you might as well have it."

I said, "Yes, but God would know the difference and I would know the difference."

It's not wrong for anybody to earn a million dollars or even more. But I know in my heart that God didn't intend for me to have a lot of money personally and that I was not to touch the gold or the glory. That was a vow I made, and I've kept it.

I admit that I have been on the edge of breaking my pledge to God. Evelyn was with me the night I nearly broke it. I sat down on the floor in our hotel room that night, and I began to weep. I cried, "Jesus, I've offended You." I hadn't done it *yet*, but I had listened to an offer and the fact that I had even entertained the idea was bad. I knew it. I knew the Lord was offended. And I knew that if I offended the Lord, I'd lose all I had to offer hurting and suffering people.

Yes, a vow is serious business. Vows should never be made

*When you
break a vow
to God,
the good news
is that you
can make
a
BETTER
vow.*

lightly or taken carelessly. Don't underestimate the power of a promise or the importance of a promise you have made. Face up to the fact that you made it.

Second, vows need to be kept with all the strength you have to keep them.

A number of years ago a man came to me and made a vow to give a certain amount of money to help build Oral Roberts University. I was not asking him for this specific gift. I was not expecting him to make this pledge to God.

Shortly after our meeting, he died in a fiery plane crash. His family came to me and asked, "Did our father promise a certain amount of money to you? He told us about a vow, and we want to know if it was true."

I said, "Yes, he made that vow. But we don't hold you to that. It was his vow, and we don't expect you to make it yours."

They said, "We'll pay it. A vow must be paid. We want God's blessing on every part of our inheritance, and we'll give what our father promised."

They did fulfill their father's pledge to God. And it has been proven to be true: Every part of their inheritance has been blessed and multiplied many times over. They proved that a good seed planted returns in a good and greater harvest.

Vows need to be kept with all of your ability to keep them. And in every case I know, this takes work. I know that my marriage vows with Evelyn have taken effort—on her part and on my part. We both must work at keeping them. Vows are not easy things to fulfill. Don't underestimate the word you've given. Don't undervalue it.

Third, if you break a vow or fail to fulfill a vow, God has a way for you to make things right.

Several years ago I had an important encounter with a partner of mine in this ministry. This man had given a great deal over the years to help spread the Gospel of Christ and to found Oral Roberts University. He had made a number of promises of financial support, and he had always kept them.

Then he made a promise for a specific project . . . and he disappeared. We didn't hear from him for about five years.

One day one of my associates called me and told me this man was in Tulsa to see Oral Roberts University and the City of Faith. I said, "Will he see me?" My associate said, "He doesn't expect to see you." I said, "Well, I expect to see him." So reluctantly, this man whom I had not seen in nearly five years came to see me.

When he came into the room, I was startled by what I saw. His face was fallen, and there was an air of sickness and despondency about him. The first thing he said was, "You remember how I used to prosper and be in health? Well, when I broke my vow, I went down and kept going down. I lost the victory. Now my marriage is falling apart, and I'm sick in my heart."

I said, "Can I pray for you?"

He said, "It won't do any good."

I said, "It will if you'll understand that God is a God of love and He will let you start over."

He said, "You mean that? You think God would let me start over?"

I said, "When Adam disobeyed God and the Fall of man occurred, God made a vow that He would send a Redeemer through the seed of the woman. He kept that vow through Noah, through Abraham, through Isaac, through Jacob, through David, and on down through Mary until Jesus Christ, our Redeemer, was born. Jesus has already been nailed to the cross. And He has risen from the dead. That means a new beginning for you and for everybody in the world. You see, God made a vow, too. He vowed that *whosoever believes in His Son, Jesus Christ, shall be saved.* He vowed to give them eternal life and to forgive them of all their sins. And His Word says, 'If we confess our sins, He is faithful and just to forgive us our sins and to cleanse us from all unrighteousness'" (1 John 1:9).

This man looked at me with huge tears welling up in his eyes. "Are you saying that God can forgive me of my broken vow and give me a second chance?"

"Yes. I don't read anywhere in my Bible that a broken vow is an unforgivable sin. God wants us to take our vows seriously.

He wants us to work with all of our strength to keep our vows and not break them. But when we do break them, He stands ready to forgive us. And when God forgives, He also forgets. He gives us a second chance to *make a better vow*."

"What do you mean, a better vow?"

"I mean you can ask forgiveness for a broken vow. You can say, 'O Lord, be merciful to me. Forgive me for breaking my word. I didn't intend to do it. Please receive me back.' And then you can make a *new vow* to God. And keep it. You can have a new beginning, and it can start right now where you are."

He and I prayed together fervently. Both he and I became convinced that he was given an exciting new chance. Over a period of time, he was.

Have you broken a vow?

Then ask God to forgive you. Be serious about it. Talk to God out of the depths of your heart and your hurt. He doesn't want you to try to live with broken promises. It's too heavy for you. Ask Him to forgive you for your failure and to help you make a new vow and keep it.

Have you lost your business? Your job? Your work?

Ask God to forgive you for any mistakes you made. Ask Him also to help you forgive yourself for your failure. And then make a new vow. Decide to have an even better business . . . a better job so that your life will count even more.

Has your marriage ended in divorce, and is all opportunity for reconciliation gone?

Ask God to forgive you for your part in that failure. Tell Him that you are sorry you've missed His ideal for your life. Make a better promise. Promise Him that you'll seek His choice of a mate for you—that you'll get in line with His perfect plan for your life and that if you are led to marry again, you'll have a good marriage. Vow that both you and your spouse will put God first in your marriage and your lives.

Have you failed with a child? Did your child stray from the way you raised him or her? Or do you feel you made mistakes that you can't go back and undo?

Ask God to forgive you for your mistakes. Forgive yourself also. Then make a new pledge to God that you'll pray for that erring child and that you'll be at peace in your heart because you've done your best.

I want to point out to you that if you *don't* ask God to forgive you for your broken vows . . . and if you *don't* forge ahead with your life and make new, better vows to the Lord, those broken vows can turn into mounting memories . . . and into an attitude that can be devastating.

Sometimes we have lousy attitudes because of failures in our lives for which we've not asked and received God's forgiveness. We almost decide within ourselves that we aren't going to try again . . . we aren't going to "conceive and believe" for any new blessings because we failed once . . . or failed many times.

Friend, if anybody ever had reason to give up, it was God. Man failed Him. God made man, and man failed. Yet God didn't give up. God sent His messengers again and again to talk to people about Him. Those methods failed. God still didn't give up. He sent Jesus. And through the gift of His Son, God is succeeding with millions in our generation . . . and will in all generations ahead. Someday we will have a new world, all because God never gives up.

Ask God to forgive you.

Make a better vow.

Ask God to help you keep it.

Then begin to conceive and believe for that vow to blossom into the greatest reality you've ever known. Now get ready to turn your faith into action—the kind of action that brings results. . . .

Consider

1. How seriously do you take the vows you have made in your life?

2. Are you weighing a decision to break a vow? Have you done everything you can to keep your vow?

3. Is there a vow that you haven't kept that you know God would like for you to start keeping? Have you asked God to help you keep your vow?

4. Have you broken a vow in your life? Have you asked God to forgive you and to give you another chance?

Choose Your Point of Contact

I almost missed praying for Willie.

The crusade services had come to a climax on that Sunday afternoon in Roanoke, Virginia. The crowd had filled the auditorium to overflowing. Almost as many people stood outside as were seated inside. I had promised earlier in the week that on the last afternoon of the crusade, I would pray for everyone I had not yet been able to pray for. Literally thousands of people passed in front of me during that final service. I was exhausted.

My clothes stuck to my body because of perspiration. It was all I could do to keep my eyes from crossing and my legs from buckling as I went backstage. I could think only one thing: *I've got to get someplace to lie down.* I was so tired even the tired people would have called me tired.

I started down the hallway that led out of the building to my car, and then I saw someone out of the corner of my eye. I walked on. But something inside me made me turn back and look again—even though I didn't see how I could have enough energy to take one extra step. I entered a room and saw Willie sitting in the corner, his head down and his crutches held up between his arms.

I didn't know it then, but Willie had been to two meetings earlier in the week. He lived about fifty miles from Roanoke—a long trip through the winding mountain roads. Each night the crowds had been so large that Willie had been too late to get a prayer card, which would have allowed him to enter the prayer line. Because of the large crowds, we had had to develop a system to control the number of people in the prayer line each night. That allowed me to have enough strength to preach and pray for an entire week of meetings.

When Willie's family came for the third time, that Sunday afternoon, it didn't appear that they would be able to get in the building. As they stood outside the main doors in the midst of the pressing crowd, Willie's mother heard an usher say something about ambulance cases arriving in the invalid room. She didn't know exactly what that meant, but she pushed her son forward. The usher began to say, "Make way for the little boy on crutches."

With great determination, Willie, his mother, and his father managed to get inside the auditorium, backstage. They stood in a corner through the service, listening to my message over a loudspeaker.

Willie had Perthes' disease. Until he was six years old, he had been a healthy, rowdy boy. But one day while playing and running through the house, he had fallen accidentally on the andirons by the fireplace. After a few days, Willie was still limping and complaining about pain in his hip. His parents took him to a doctor, but he didn't find anything wrong other than a serious bruise.

Willie's parents followed the doctor's recommendations for treating the pain and the bruise, but Willie's situation didn't improve. They took Willie to a nearby hospital. By this time, in just a matter of weeks, his leg had shortened by two and a half inches, and he couldn't walk without assistance. The doctor at the hospital diagnosed Perthes' disease—flattening of the hipbone—and put Willie into traction. There was no improvement. Eventually the doctors devised a built-up shoe and leg brace for Willie and fitted him with crutches. Willie was a cripple.

Now he was backstage in a Roanoke auditorium . . . the service over . . . the press of the crowds had been so great . . . and

You can set
the time, place,
and circumstances
for releasing your
faith to God . . .
for getting your
miracle under way.

Only God determines
when your miracle
will be completed.
But you can determine
when it begins!

Choose a
Point of Contact
today!

Willie had not been prayed for. He was sitting in the corner of this out-of-the-way room, waiting. Just waiting. And I was walking out. Some invisible force had brought us together.

"Son," I asked, "what are you doing in here?"

"Waiting for Oral Roberts."

"I'm Oral Roberts."

"You are?" His eyes were wide as saucers.

"Yes. What do you want?"

"Well, I'm supposed to be healed today."

"Son, I don't have any strength left to pray."

He said, "I don't know about that . . . but I'm *supposed* to be healed today."

"What's your name?"

"Willie."

I said, "Do you believe Jesus can heal you, Willie?"

"Uh-huh," Willie said and nodded his head yes.

I said, "Willie, I'm out of strength. I'll touch you in Jesus' name, but you'll have to do the believing."

He said, "Okay."

Under my breath, I said, "God, heal Willie." And I walked out.

Several weeks later I received word of what had happened. That night when Willie got home, he said, "Dad, get across the room. Mom, take my crutches." He pulled off the big built-up shoe, took off his brace, and said, "Dad, I'm going to walk to you."

Well, Willie didn't walk.

He ran!

Without the slightest limp, he rushed into his father's arms across the room. In the hours since the prayer, both legs had become the same length, and his legs were restored. Willie had received his miracle!

The next day Willie was late for school. You see, he had made his parents promise him that if he was healed on Sunday, he could have a new pair of shoes on Monday. Willie was up at the crack of dawn on Monday morning—no need for an alarm clock that day. He and his mother were at the shoe store exactly when it opened, and by ten o'clock Willie was walking into his classroom.

The teacher had quite a time calming down the class that day, with everybody rushing around Willie and cheering.

From that day on, Willie has lived a normal life. I've heard from him regularly through the years. He and his daddy love to hunt deer together in the mountains of Virginia. In fact, Willie has won a number of trophies for his hunting skill. And let me tell you, it takes a good pair of legs to trudge up and down those trails of the Blue Ridge Mountains outside his hometown.

One thing stands out about Willie's story that is vital to you and to every person who is trying to recover from something bad.

Willie had a *Point of Contact*.

What is a Point of Contact?

A Point of Contact is something you do . . . and when you do it, you release your faith to God.

It's like turning on a light switch. You *expect* the lights to come on when you flip the switch. You know the switch is connected to the power company.

When you use a Point of Contact, you are *doing something to trigger the release of your faith*.

You are literally setting the time and place and situation in which you are going to release your faith. You choose your Point of Contact. It's something *you* do.

When my son Richard was just a boy, he developed warts on his left hand. Twenty-two of them, to be exact. At first, Richard wasn't bothered by the appearance of the warts. He was a rough-and-tumble, torn T-shirt, dirt-on-his-face boy, and the warts didn't keep him from fishing or playing ball. Eventually, though, Evelyn noticed that the warts were growing and seemed to be spreading. She said to Richard one day, "We need to go to the doctor and have these burned off."

Suddenly, the warts became a very serious matter to Richard. He was not the least bit interested in experiencing the pain and discomfort that seemed to loom ahead. In the midst of his protests, Evelyn promised that he could wait to see the doctor until after my next visit home. During that time I was on the road a great deal with the crusades, usually spending up to three weeks a month in great crusade meetings that touched every major city of America and many nations overseas.

On my next trip home, Richard and I confronted the warts. We went to his room, and I said, "Now, Richard, when I put my hand on your hand and pray, I want you to turn your faith loose to God."

"Turn my faith loose?"

"Yes. Do you see that light switch over there on the wall?"

"Yes."

"Well, the light switch is connected to the power company. And when you flip on the light switch, it causes the electricity from the power company to come surging into the room and make the lights go on."

Richard just stared at the light switch.

"Now when I lay my hand on yours, I want you to send your faith up to God just that way."

"Okay."

I knew that Richard and his younger sister Roberta had often heard me preach and pray for the sick over the radio. That's one of the ways they stayed close to this ministry all their growing-up years. They'd listen to the broadcasts of the crusade services. And often as we closed those broadcasts I'd ask the people to touch their radio sets—and later their television sets—as a Point of Contact for the releasing of their faith. I was asking them to use this same principle.

Richard and I held hands, and I prayed, "God, heal these warts on Richard's hand. In the Name of Jesus. Amen."

Richard opened his eyes and looked up at the ceiling of the room, and with a wide motion of his hands upward and downward, he began to say, "Faith, get up to God. Faith, get up to God. Faith, get up to God."

And that's really what a Point of Contact does. It gives you a place and time when *you are saying by what you are doing:* Faith, get up to God.

Richard looked down at his hand, and the warts were still there. But within a matter of days, they began to shrink. Soon they were entirely gone. The Point of Contact Richard used had become the turnaround point in his road to recovery.

Think about it for a moment. All sources of power have a point of contact through which they can be reached or tapped. You turn the key to your automobile to start the motor. You turn a faucet to get water. A person flips a switch that starts the rockets that hurl our space shuttle into space. In each case, what an individual does to start the flow of energy becomes the Point of Contact.

You may ask, "Is the Point of Contact in the Bible?"

The Bible abounds with examples of men and women who used a Point of Contact to release their faith to bring deliverance to themselves and others.

David used his *slingshot,* and as he did, he released his faith and killed Goliath.

Moses raised his *rod,* and as he did, he released his faith and the Red Sea rolled back.

Elijah let his faith go to God when he struck the water with his *mantle* and the waters divided.

One blind man had his eyes anointed with *clay,* and he used that to release his faith and was healed by Jesus.

The Roman centurion used the *spoken word of Jesus* as his Point of Contact for the healing of his servant. The moment he heard Jesus "speak the word," it triggered his faith.

The synagogue leader, Jairus, witnessed *Jesus' hands* touching his little daughter—they became his Point of Contact to cause his faith to go to God for her to be raised up.

Hundreds used *handkerchiefs and aprons* that the Apostle Paul had prayed over for their Point of Contact as they touched their bodies. Others used the passing of Peter's *shadow* over them as the time to release their faith for their healing.

In my own ministry through the years, I have asked my partners to *do* many things as a Point of Contact to get them to release their faith.

Under the inspiration of the Holy Spirit, I asked one woman to run up and down an aisle seven times. She did. She was healed.

I have asked countless persons to bend over three times . . . or to touch the chair of the person in front of them . . . or to take the hand of the person next to them . . . or to return something in the mail to me . . . or to touch themselves.

Why?

Because the only way I know to get your faith into motion is to *do something* that is tangible, that is a specific act, that is an identifiable moment in time with which you can relate.

It doesn't make any difference what *your* Point of Contact is. God will honor any Point of Contact that will help you release your faith. The important thing is not what you do, but the fact that you do it. And when you do it, you release your faith to Him for your healing or some other benefit.

One woman wrote to me a number of years ago that as she was lying in bed, listening to our radio broadcast, she heard me ask those in need of healing to touch their radios as a Point of Contact. She prayed, "Lord, You know that I'm ready to be healed, but I can't reach the radio. So I'm going to let this refrigerator next to my bed be my Point of Contact." She wrote that she received her miracle.

Let me repeat it: A Point of Contact is something *you* select and *choose* to do. It may be going to a specific meeting. It may be touching a particular object, such as placing your hand on a particular Scripture in the Word of God. It may be having a certain person come to pray for you or your going to that person. It may be making a telephone call to a prayer group. It may be holding on to this book right *now* and, as you do so, choosing to release your faith to God.

A Point of Contact sets the time.

Suppose I said to you, "I'd like to meet you."

And you said, "Fine, Oral Roberts, when?"

And I said, "Oh, anytime."

And you said, "Where?"

And I said, "Oh, anywhere."

Let me assure you that you and I would never meet.

But now suppose I said to you, "I will meet you."

And you said, "Where?"

And I said, "In my office at three o'clock tomorrow afternoon." Well, then, the time and place would be set. We'd likely meet.

A Point of Contact does not set the time, necessarily, for your healing or your miracle to be completed. That's most important for you to understand. God alone holds the timetable for meeting your need. But a Point of Contact does set the time for the *releasing* of your faith. There's one thing you must learn: Your faith in your heart is important, but you must release it to God if it is to work. Doing this doesn't mean your faith is taken away or lost. It means it becomes active. It also means your faith grows by your using it.

Willie had done that. He believed he was *supposed to be healed* that Sunday afternoon in Roanoke. He set himself to believe that when a man named Oral Roberts touched him and prayed for him, that moment was the start of his healing. He didn't take the brace off and run right away. That came later at his home. But he released his faith to God in that out-of-the-way room, backstage of an empty auditorium, when an exhausted man of God whispered a prayer that probably wasn't heard by anybody but Willie and God.

When you use your Point of Contact, it *starts* the miracle-working process. It's up to God—and God alone—how long that process takes and when it is completed. *You alone* set the starting process. *God alone* sets the schedule and completion date.

Finally, a Point of Contact is really a way of touching Jesus.

The woman in Luke 8 who had an issue of blood for twelve years—an uncontrollable hemorrhage that the doctors couldn't help her with—sought out Jesus. She didn't have any idea that Jesus would touch her. According to the Jewish customs, she was "unclean"—an outcast—and anyone who touched her would also become unclean. No righteous man would have touched her, and she knew Jesus was the most righteous man she had ever heard about. No, this woman had no thought that Jesus would touch *her*. But she also believed that Jesus was her only hope. She had gone from doctor to doctor to doctor all those years. Every one of them had tried to help her, but nothing had worked. Her life was literally ebbing from her body, day by day. She needed a miracle, and she knew she needed one soon.

She decided to touch Jesus. She decided that if she could just crawl through the crowd, moving along at foot level, she might be unnoticed by the crowd. Then she could reach out and touch Jesus' robe as He passed by. The hem of Jesus' garment was her Point of Contact. *She* chose it. She decided it would be that. She decided that touching His robe would put her faith into action. She decided that her faith would be released at the time of her touch. And most of all, she decided that touching Jesus' garment was just as good as touching Jesus or having Him touch her.

"But," you say, "she was dealing with the actual Jesus in the flesh, who was walking and talking and preaching and healing on the earth. It's almost two thousand years later."

Well, I believe in a *now* Christ. I believe that if He ever healed anybody, He's healing people today. If He ever saved anybody, He's saving people today. If people could reach out with their faith toward Him then, they can do it today.

Fred O'Dell knows what I mean.

In January of 1955 Fred started to get sick. Within thirty days he had lost twenty-nine pounds, and he wasn't dieting. He was ill. After two weeks of medical examinations, the doctors told Fred the verdict. He had cancer of the lymph glands, and it had spread to both lungs. The disease was so advanced that surgery was impossible. They gave him six months to live, a year at the longest.

Heartbroken, Fred and his wife went to the church he pastored and asked the members to pray for him. They did, and as they were praying, Fred's wife felt an overwhelming impression to take Fred to one of my crusades.

Fred had been to one of my meetings a few weeks earlier, not far from where he lived in California. He had resented what I taught about God wanting His people to prosper in every area of their lives. He, like Evelyn and me, had been taught that a person had to be poor to be Christian. But now Fred's circumstances had changed. He was in desperate need of a miracle, and he later wrote me, "I was in no mood to argue with anyone."

By this time, however, I had gone from California clear across the nation to Jacksonville, Florida—2,904 miles away.

Fred and his wife traveled by car for five days to get to Jacksonville. And for the next five days he sat through every service, hearing me preach, hearing my associate evangelist, Bob DeWeese. With every service, Fred's faith began to become more and more alive within him. He became more and more aware of his faith.

Choosing a Point of Contact makes you more aware of the power of your faith and the fact that you have faith. The Bible says that God has given every person the "measure of faith" (Rom. 12:3). You don't go out and get faith somewhere; you already have it. The real key issue is: What are you *doing* with your faith?

One man said to me, "I have all the faith in the world."

"Well," I said, "why are you coming to *me* for prayer?" Then I said, "You know, that's really your trouble."

He looked at me with a puzzled expression. "What do you mean?"

I said, "The trouble is that although you have all that faith, it's lying inactive in your spirit. It isn't enough to have your faith, you have to *release* it to the Lord."

A person can have all the money in the world and still starve to death if he doesn't release a little of it to buy food. A person can have a full plate of food sitting right in front of him and *still* starve to death if he doesn't make the effort to eat any of it. You've got to *do* something. God Himself says, "Faith without works is dead" (James 2:20). It gets you nowhere.

"Well," you might say, "I've lost my faith."

Not many people have really lost their faith. When a person says that, he's usually saying, "I've not been using my faith," or "I've not been releasing my faith," or "I'm discouraged." It isn't easy to lose the measure of faith God has put into one's spirit. With all the people I've dealt with, touching more than a million with my right hand and praying for their healing, I don't remember meeting a one who I believed had lost his faith.

You might say, "Well, I accept the fact I have faith, but how do I build up my faith?" In the same way that Fred did there in Jacksonville. You've got to open your Bible, begin reading and studying it so that you get into the Word of God with your spirit and mind. This is so vital that I tell persons who are blind to listen to the Bible on tape or have someone read it to them. Then you've got to hear the Word of God preached to you.

The Bible tells us that "faith comes by hearing . . . the word of God" (Rom. 10:17). This is why God calls and anoints certain men and women to preach and teach His Word. You've got to "hear" it for your faith to become alive and active . . . and be in position for you to release it to God. Believe me, you'll never find a substitute for hearing the Word of God preached and taught.

If you're not attending a Bible-believing church where the Word of God is preached with power and builds up your faith . . . find one. Get active in it.

Get involved with tapes . . . records . . . television programs and radio programs that preach the Gospel to you in your home. They are all available resources for you to build up your faith to the point where it almost bursts out of you as you release it.

The time finally came for Fred to be in the prayer line. We were taping that night for television in the big tent so we have an actual transcript of what happened when Fred and I met for the first time on that stage in front of the Jacksonville audience. This is what happened:

ORAL: What is wrong with you, Fred?

FRED: Well, the doctors say I have incurable cancer of the lymph glands and it is all over my body—they say that I have had it about eight months.

ORAL: You know, a lot of people don't stop to realize that the almighty God is able to heal cancer. He is fully able to do it. We need to believe and to turn our faith to God. Fred, I am going to pray for you now, and I know this great audience will have compassion and pray with me.

Oh, God, I bring this young man from Oakland, California, to Thee tonight—not in my name but in the Name of Jesus of Nazareth, the Son of the living God. Hear Thy servant's prayer and heal him—heal the lymph glands from cancer that it shall leave his body in the Name of Jesus of Nazareth.

Well, the power of God is so strong tonight. Fred, look up here at me a minute, please. Why were you trembling so violently?

FRED: I don't know.

ORAL: Well, Fred, it is possible to feel the presence of God.

FRED: I know it is.

ORAL: People in Bible days felt that presence, and they did exploits.

FRED: I know it.

ORAL: You came here to be healed, didn't you?

FRED: Yes. I got it.

ORAL: Well, we trust that you have because it is God that heals and you feel His presence very strongly, don't you?

FRED: Oh, yes.

ORAL: God bless you as you go back to Oakland with your wife and may you be completely healed in Christ's name.

Then I prayed a second time for Fred, and this time he became completely engulfed by the Holy Spirit. With his spiritual eyesight, Fred no longer saw my hand touching him. He saw the hand of Jesus from the elbows down. The hands of Jesus seemed to be placed over his forehead and downward over his body, and he saw the nailprint there and the blood running from Jesus' hand. In *human* reality, there was a man named Oral Roberts who was touching a man named Fred O'Dell and praying for his healing. In *spiritual* reality, there was a Man named Jesus, the Son of almighty God, who was reaching down to touch Fred's life in a way that he would never be the same.

Soon the terrible stench of the cancer left Fred's body. His appetite, which had been ravenous, became normal again.

Fred went back home to California and soon had the strength to return to work. He faithfully continued going to his doctor for checkups as I had instructed him. The cancer disappeared *over time*—and within six months all the symptoms were gone. The X-rays verified that the cancer had completely disappeared. The doctors said, "Fred, all we can say is that it appears to be a miracle!"

Recently, I heard from Fred again. He's still in the ministry, leading a busy life serving God as a pastor and an evangelist, and is still well and strong. His healing from cancer has lasted more than thirty years.

Yes, Fred knows what it means to select a Point of Contact and reach out to touch Jesus and be touched by Him.

Countless other people have shared with me experience after experience after experience that all lead to the same conclusion: They *did* something with their faith as an act of reaching out to touch Jesus. And when they did, His power came into their lives . . . sometimes slowly, sometimes fast . . . sometimes as a growing tide, sometimes as a flood . . . sometimes with dramatic, visible results, sometimes with a quiet knowing that becomes a fact days or even months later.

What about you?

What will you choose to *do* as your Point of Contact?

Will you get into the Word of God . . . will you hear the Word preached so your faith will become strong and active . . . will you select a Point of Contact that you feel good about . . . will you *do* something to release your faith?

Will you choose your Point of Contact to set the time?

What will you choose that will cause you to expect your miracle to begin to happen?

Will you use your Point of Contact as a way of touching Jesus? Will you see Him as the focal point of your Point of Contact?

A woman stopped me outside the back of an auditorium one time and literally demanded that I pray for her. As usual after ministering to a crowd of ten thousand or more people, I was exhausted and eager to get back to my hotel room.

I admit I resented her approach of almost assaulting me to get me to pray.

Finally, I whirled and said to her, "Woman, I'm so tired I don't have any faith for *you* to be healed."

She grabbed my coat, and as I was trying to get it loose from her grasp, she suddenly released it. With a cry, she began thanking God for healing her.

I was astonished at her simple but brazen act. Like another woman two thousand years before, she had seized that moment to be her Point of Contact. She wasn't going to be denied it. Although she made me angry, she was releasing her faith and getting the result she came for.

Back in my room I began to feel ashamed at my reaction to her. God took that moment to teach me a lesson. In my spirit I heard Him say, "I healed her, but you won't get any credit for it."

I wept and repented . . . and learned.

Don't let anything keep *you* from acting on your Point of Contact.

Don't just talk about it . . . do it.

Don't just plan it . . . act on it.

Don't just wish for it . . . *make it happen!*

Consider

1. Have you decided to reach out and touch Jesus for the miracle you need?

2. *What* will *you* choose as *your* Point of Contact for the releasing of *your* faith to God? When?

3. Are you *using* your faith or is it lying dormant within you?

4. How are you building up your own faith?

Get Into a Rhythm of Planting Seeds of Your Faith

What is faith? One of the best definitions I've ever heard is one my son Richard uses as he preaches the Word of God and prays for the healing of the sick on his live daily TV program nationwide:

Faith is what you hold onto until you get what you believe for.

I asked him, "Richard, what do you mean?"

He said, "Well, Dad, faith has staying power. It has endurance, and that's what can steady us until we reach the point where we can release our faith to God."

I agree. There's something about faith that calls for it to be put into action . . . again and again and again and again. It isn't enough to set a Point of Contact once and then let your faith lie dormant. The Point of Contact is the beginning. Your faith must continue to be planted . . . day after day after day after day.

I've discovered that faith follows the rhythm that God put into this universe—the rhythm of seedtime and harvest.

I first confronted God's principles of seedtime and harvest in a major way while I was a young pastor and university student. It seemed that Evelyn and I were living on the very brink of poverty all the time. One week we faced my tuition payments, the next week our car needed repair, the next week we needed additional groceries or clothes, and every week we dedicated our tithe—the ten percent—to give to God.

More often than I care to remember, Evelyn and I would find

ourselves at the cash register stand, and I had to take certain items back to the shelves so that we could pay the amount owed. This never failed to embarrass me. I felt everybody was looking at us. And the fact that I preached the Gospel and was supposed to be a model of God's promise to supply all the needs of His children made me look even worse. I lived with low self-esteem about my relationship with God and my faith that He would supply my needs.

At the same time I was preaching week after week that God wanted to heal sick bodies and have us live triumphantly over the devil. When I attempted to apply the Word of God to the *material* needs that I knew the people had, the words seemed to stick in my throat.

Then one day the board of our little church and I sat down and figured up the absolute minimum required for me and my family to exist. I included groceries, car expenses, clothes, even a haircut twice a month. We figured it almost to the penny. In 1947 it came to fifty-five dollars a week.

For the next several weeks we squeezed by, but resentment grew in my heart. No matter how much I gave my tithes and served the church—and I was on call day and night, my whole life outside the hours I spent in the university was engaged with the people of this church—I was locked into fifty-five dollars a week. No matter how well I preached . . . no matter how many people were saved . . . no matter how many new members joined the church . . . fifty-five dollars a week.

One day something from the Word of God dawned on me: I realized that the board of that church was not my source of supply. God was. God *wanted* to meet my needs. I needed to take the lid off my faith. I needed to stop praying for the board to give me a raise. I needed to start looking to God who promised to supply all my needs according to *His riches,* not according to the meager resources of that little church. I needed to see that this group was only an *instrument* or a means that God would use. They were not my source; God was.

That's a very important difference for you to understand as you confront the needs of your life and recover from the blows that strike you.

To reap a harvest
of miracles,
you must
first plant
a seed
of your faith
—time, love,
money,
energy, an act
of kindness.

Plant out of
your need.
Sow for a
desired result.
Give God something
to work with!

A source is not an instrument. An instrument is not a source.

God alone is the Source of your supply in life. Everything else is an instrument.

While I was growing up, we lived close to an uncle who had a big peach orchard. In his later life it was my privilege to lead him to Christ. We spent many happy hours together when I was a boy helping him gather the peaches to sell. It was he who first helped me to see the difference between a source and an instrument.

My uncle raised many types of fruit—but his pride and joy was the big, luscious Elberta peach. People came from miles around to buy peaches from him.

After I entered the ministry, I moved away from that area, and it was several years before I visited my uncle again. I was shocked to see what had happened to the orchard, or what remained of it. Gone were most of the beautiful fruit-growing trees. Only one or two trees of the prized Elberta peach remained. They were stubby and produced only a few small peaches.

"What happened?" I asked my uncle. "Did you have a storm?"

"No."

"An invasion of insects?"

"No."

"Some type of fruit-tree disease?"

"No, Oral," he said. "It wasn't any of that. It was me."

"What did you do?" I asked.

Sadly he replied, "I'll tell you what happened. As long as the fruit came each fall, I was satisfied to leave the trees alone. They bore fruit, and I thought my supply was the fruit. The sale of the fruit fed my family. We sold thousands of bushels. And we used the money to buy the things we needed. The fruit became everything to me. I depended upon it. Everything I did, I judged according to how it related to the fruit.

"Then one year the crop was not so good. The next year it was less. That was when I stopped thinking about fruit and started looking to the trees. Before, I had paid little attention to the trees. Oh, I cut the weeds and did a little plowing down each row. But I hadn't paid serious attention to them. I hadn't *focused* my attention on them.

"It suddenly hit me. The peaches and other fruit were just that—fruit of the tree. The supply source was the tree. If I took care of the tree, the fruit would grow. Because of my neglect, I have only these few poor trees left. There's not even enough fruit to bother picking anymore."

But then my uncle's eyes lighted up. He said, "Now I'm putting in a young orchard. I've gone to the agricultural experts and learned how to take care of the tree first. I'm starting over. And this time I'll take care of the source of the fruit."

As I thought back over what my uncle had said, I realized that I had been doing the same thing with my church. I had looked to the results—my fifty-five-dollar-a-week salary—as my source rather than to God. The people who helped me were instruments, but they were not my source.

My resentment left. I knew God could make a way for Oral Roberts and his family. I knew God controlled all the means of supply, both expected and unexpected.

Then I came face-to-face with a verse in the Bible that can change your entire life if you'll catch hold of its meaning: "Give, and it will be given to you: good measure, pressed down . . . and running over" (Luke 6:38).

I decided to see if God meant what He said. If He was my Source of supply, and if He said that His method was for us to give to Him and He would cause our giving to come back to us, then I needed to see if that verse really meant what it said.

I don't know of any *direct* way to give to God. I've never figured out a way to just reach up and give something out of my hand directly into God's hand in heaven. I can give God my praise—and I do—but when it comes to giving anything tangible that's here on earth, whether it's money or some object or my time or my abilities, I haven't found a way to deliver it personally to God.

How do we give then? We give to people who are doing things on the earth that are a part of God's plan and that are a part of God's work. We give to projects that are extensions of the work of Jesus—projects that get people saved and healed and delivered, projects that allow people to grow in the Lord and prosper as His people.

And that's exactly what I decided to do during the Wednesday night prayer meeting at my church. A pressing need was facing the church, and it was a need that was going to ultimately be solved because people gave money. So I stood up and said, "As you all know, Evelyn and I give ten percent of our salary to the church each Sunday. But something's not working. I feel tonight that in addition to our tithes I must give my entire week's salary . . . all fifty-five dollars of it."

This Scripture—Luke 6:38—was alive in my mind. I acted on it impulsively and cheerfully. After the service I went home feeling so good I felt as if I was walking on air.

Evelyn said, "Oral!"

To put it mildly, she wasn't enthusiastic about what I had done. She let me know in no uncertain terms that I had just given away our food money and that if the children starved, it was my fault.

We both had a hard time getting to sleep that night.

And then a knock came at the door. It was early in the morning—well past midnight—and somebody was pounding on the door.

I went to see who it was. A man who hadn't been coming to our church very long was there, and he said, "Brother Roberts, can I come in?" I invited him in from the wintry, icy cold.

He said, "I felt bad tonight at church because I didn't give anything. I'm a wheat farmer, and I know you've got to plant wheat to get wheat. I went home and was under conviction because God had impressed me to give and I wouldn't do it. I went to bed, but I was so restless I got up and went out into the yard where I had buried some money. The Lord told me to plant it by giving it to you."

He handed me some money and walked out.

When I unfolded it, I found four hundred-dollar bills.

I turned around, and there was Evelyn, peering around the

corner of the bedroom door. I waved those bills and said, "See! What did I tell you? God is our Source. He answers prayer. When we give, He will give back to us just like Jesus says in Luke 6:38 that I've been studying."

I had given fifty-five dollars, and now God had multiplied it. I had seven times as much right there in my hand.

In the days that followed, the parting words of this man rang in my ears. He had said, "Brother Roberts, this is just seed I've been needing to plant for a long time."

That was the first time I had heard the word *seed* linked to giving. This man had showed me the link by comparing the giving of his money to the planting of seeds. *The money was a seed of his faith that God was going to meet the needs of his life.* I knew this concept was the Word of God. I also instantly knew that what I was learning that night would change my life and the lives of many more in the years ahead.

Today I call it SEED-FAITH. It's giving something . . . planting something . . . putting something into the good soil of God's work. And when you plant that seed, you wrap it up with your faith that God is going to take care of you. He's going to meet your need . . . carry you through . . . help you . . . deliver you . . . be the Source of your total supply.

It's funny how people can catch hold of this idea when they plant their vegetable gardens . . . or when they invest their money in a money-market fund . . . or when they reach out a hand to someone to shake it friendly-like. They know they are planting seeds, and what they plant will be multiplied back to them. Yet they find it difficult to understand that the Word of God teaches that our love and our faith are seeds we are to sow in the form of giving our money, our abilities, our time and efforts. What we are learning through actual practice is that the Bible's teaching on giving and receiving, seedtime and harvest, sowing and reaping (all meaning the same thing), is God's very same eternal principle that works in every area of our lives—spiritual, physical, financial.

My friend, Art Neufield, who came to my door with his four hundred-dollar bills as seeds, was doing the same thing spiritually for God to meet his needs as he was when he planted his wheat seeds in the spring to receive his wheat harvests in late summer or early fall. He knew he had to sow in order to reap, and he had to sow—or give—*first*.

Notice that you breathe out, then you breathe in. You must breathe out in order to breath in. God put this principle of giving and receiving in everything, including your breathing.

You give to God, then you expect to receive back from God. You breathe out, you breathe in. You sow and you are to reap— you sow and you are to receive back from God your Source.

Giving is the very essence of our lives in relationship to God. As people who call ourselves Christians, we should be the biggest givers of all. We should also be the biggest receivers.

Giving and receiving are a rhythm . . . the rhythm of life itself.

Notice again that you breathe out and you breathe in. You breathe in so you can breathe out again. And again. And again.

A farmer sows and reaps his harvest, and then he plants again. He gets into a rhythm of it. It's always again and again and again.

We give to God. We receive back. Why? So we can give again. So we can receive again, give again, receive again—a rhythm that gives essence, the essential elements, to our lives on earth.

That's one of the reasons I've preached all these years that we can never give too much to God and we can never receive too much from God. They are in balance. They form a circle that is continuous and continual. Giving and receiving. Receiving and giving. It's a rhythm of using our faith and keeping our faith alive and strong so that we make things happen.

Let me share with you three important things I've learned about giving.

First, give out of your need. If you need money, give money. If you need love, give love. If you need a friendly smile, give a friendly smile. If you need prayer, sow prayer. You make something happen when you give of the very thing you need. It opens you up inside to the way God works. You get in a guaranteed position to receive back. I don't know all the mystery of it. I just know that it works that way.

Recently at a freshman orientation meeting at Oral Roberts University, I spoke about this to the students. Afterwards, a girl rushed up to me and said, "Oh, President Roberts, since I've come on campus everything is in such a rush that I just don't have any time."

I said, "Have you thought of giving some seedtime to God?"

She replied, "Oh, I'm so busy going to class and getting oriented to everything that I have no time to give."

I said, "Don't you have fifteen minutes out of the whole day you could give?"

She said, "Well, I guess so. But how do I give it?"

I said, "How about giving it to some other freshman who is frantic, also? Or go to a professor and ask him to give you something to do to help him with his class. Or go to the chaplain and offer fifteen minutes to help prepare to serve the spiritual needs of the students."

She said, "But how will this help me with my time?"

I said, "Remember, God is *the* Source of all your time. Every minute of every day that you live is something that comes to you directly from God. Give these few minutes each day as a seed for God to multiply back in more time for you. Ask Him to renew your time constantly."

Students catch on quickly. I saw she was getting the point. I said, "It's SEED-FAITH for the time miracle you need."

The following week I went to the Prayer Tower that's in the center of the Oral Roberts University campus. There this freshman was serving as a tour guide. She said, "President Roberts, I've got good news! I did what you said, and now the Lord is giving me all the time I need. I'm not rushed anymore. I've attended every class and made every assignment, and I still find time to work here in the Prayer Tower several hours a week. It's a miracle!"

This young woman still had twenty-four hours a day just like all the rest of us. But something had happened in her life and in her use of time. The time she gave to God by investing it . . .

planting it . . . seeding it into the things of God . . . was blessed. The time she had left was also blessed by God! It seemed to be multiplied to her. She was getting more done in less time than she had previously thought possible. Things were moving more smoothly. Her outlook was different. She no longer had a time need.

This young woman had given out of her need. She had received back the very thing she needed.

Second, plant your seeds of faith in the best soil you can find. You know what that means in the natural world. It takes the right kind of soil to grow prize-winning tomatoes or any other fruit or vegetable.

The same is true in the spiritual realm. Find the places where your seeds have the greatest potential to do the most good. Don't just scatter your seeds of faith at random. *Plant* them, but select the place or the way to plant them.

My thousands of partners and I plant our seeds in many different places, including the churches we are part of. We've also planted to build Oral Roberts University. We've continued to plant seeds there for the twenty-one years of its existence. Why? Because it's fertile soil. When you plant your faith into the lives of young people who can go and do and preach and teach around the world, you are extending yourself beyond your own lifetime and into areas where you can never go!

God commanded me to build Oral Roberts University. I obeyed. But I have obeyed with a sense of joy because I know I'm planting my life—which is made up of my time, my energy, my talents, my earnings—into fertile soil. I'm a part of something that's alive and great in the now . . . and that's going to be left behind in this world to continue to do a mighty work for the furtherance of the Gospel. All the young preachers, physicians, dentists, nurses, lawyers, teachers, business leaders, and others in many fields will outlive me and my partners— and God has assured me their work will exceed ours. That is fertile soil.

One of our newspaper editors here in Tulsa wrote one time that you don't need to look very far to see where Oral Roberts puts the money he receives from his partners. It's obvious. Just look at Oral Roberts University.

But ORU isn't the only place we continue to plant seeds. We have seeded for the City of Faith Health-Care Center because it's putting prayer and medicine together—it's joining God's healing streams of medical science and powerful prayer to create one of the most effective healing forces on the earth today. It's doing God's work. It's extending the healing ministry of Jesus to thousands who never before have had the opportunity to see what the best of medicine and the best of prayer can do for their wellness . . . their wholeness.

We plant seeds in our local churches. What would any of us do without local churches, or how can God's work continue in our communities without them?

We plant seeds in other ministries as the Lord leads us. They are doing good work for the Lord. They are fertile soil.

It's up to *you* to decide where you will plant . . . where you will give . . . and which soil has the greatest potential for yielding a harvest. The important thing is to decide, then do it.

And third, give for a desired result. A farmer who wants wheat is going to plant wheat seed. And the minute he plants, he starts expecting that seed to grow . . . to shoot forth, to grow up, to bear more wheat.

It's here that I find so many people having a difficult time. They really have a hard time expecting to receive back from God. Yet it is the most natural thing in the world if they will only obey the Word of God.

For one thing, they've been taught that it's wrong to receive anything back. They've been told it's wrong to expect back from God. They get confused by comparing *receiving* with *getting*. But when used in the scriptural sense, *receiving* and *getting* mean the same thing.

That's the message of perhaps the most widely known verse in the entire Bible: "For God so loved the world that He gave His only begotten Son, that whoever believes in Him should not perish but have everlasting life" (John 3:16).

Notice the word *that*. He gave . . . *that* whoever believes. He gave *in order, so that, because He anticipated that* whoever believes should have everlasting life.

God gave Jesus to get something . . . to get a desired result. It was to get man back. God had lost man in the Garden of Eden when a man chose his own way over God's way, disobeyed, and separated himself from God. God had a burning desire to get man back. Jesus was the *seed*. In fact, early in the Bible, God referred to Jesus as the seed when He made a promise to Eve: "The seed of the woman shall bruise the heel of the serpent" (see Gen. 3:15).

Yes, God planted Jesus into this earth. He planted His life at Calvary. They planted His body in a tomb owned by another man, Joseph of Arimathaea. And God did it for the most precious desired result: you . . . me . . . us. God did it to get us back into a right relationship with Himself so that He might bless us.

Now if God planted Jesus for a desired result, what makes you think that you shouldn't plant for a desired result? Is it because you haven't been taught it yet? Are you using the word *get* in the wrong sense?

My friend, Dr. Myron Sackett, discovered this principle of God in a dramatic way. Originally, though, he found it difficult to think of receiving back from God's hand. Then something happened that changed his thinking.

Dr. Sackett was associated with me in the ministry for about fifteen years before he died in the early 1970s. He was in charge of our project to print and make available Hebrew Bibles in Israel.

I have always had a great love for Israel and the Jewish people. By the time I met Dr. Sackett I had met with David Ben-Gurion twice, as well as the mayor of Jerusalem and other top officials in Israel. I had negotiated with them a way to get the complete Bible—both Old Testament and New Testament—into fairly wide circulation in Israel. They had agreed that *if* we printed the Bibles in Hebrew, they would put them in the libraries, schools, and other government places as a way of getting the people to relearn the Hebrew language. I dreamed of printing one hundred thousand copies of the Bible for Israel. Dr. Sackett had a similar dream.

At the time I met Dr. Sackett he had spent nearly every dollar he had to print a few Bibles and ship them to Israel.

I asked him, "Are you willing to make a covenant with God for your life?"

"Yes," he said.

"Are you willing to undertake this project of Bibles for Israel with me?"

"Yes. What do we do first?"

"I want you to give me one hundred dollars."

He said, "Why?"

"I need it for the Lord's work."

He said, "Sure, I'll give you a hundred dollars."

Then I said, "I want you to give me the hundred dollars on the condition that you will *expect* God to multiply it back into *your* hand."

He said, "Oh, I can't do that. But I'll give you the hundred dollars."

I said, "Why won't you expect to receive back from God?"

"Because," he said, "I've always been taught when I give not to expect anything back."

"Then I won't accept your hundred dollars."

"You won't?"

"No. I can get along without your hundred dollars, Dr. Sackett, but I'm going to tell you something, and you'd better listen to what I'm about to say because I feel the anointing power of God. I've been taught by the same teachers you've had. But there's a chapter in the Bible that has a lot to say about giving and receiving *back*. I want you to take this chapter and really study it. Read it, and hear what God is saying to your *spirit*. Then come back to me."

The chapter I gave to Dr. Sackett was 1 Kings 17. This is one of the great chapters in the Bible about faith in terms of understanding the power of sowing and reaping, seedtime and harvest, giving and receiving. This chapter tells how the great prophet Elijah challenged a poverty-stricken widow to take a risk of faith by giving, then expecting to receive back from God.

I encourage you to get your Bible and read that chapter today. Notice two things. First, notice the prophet Elijah.

Elijah was on the run. He was fleeing for his life from the authorities. God had given him a message for the wicked King Ahab and his queen, Jezebel, that there wouldn't be any rain in the land until Elijah pronounced it to fall. And for many months, there had been no rain.

God directed Elijah to a stream. There, every morning Elijah would wake up and come out of the cave and look up because he was expecting a miracle from the hand of God, his Source. He had to have a miracle. He couldn't do without one. He didn't know what instrument God would use, but he knew God had to do something. And out in front of that cave, Elijah looked up one day to see ravens flying by. They dropped food for him to eat, and they did this daily for some time.

Do you know where the most likely place in all the land would have been for those ravens to have found food in the midst of that type of famine and drought? King Ahab's palace.

Friend, we must never try to guess how God is going to supply us the miracle we need. He has every available means at His fingertips! These include ones we haven't thought of yet.

Then the brook dried up, and the ravens stopped coming. Isn't that just the way it is sometimes? You have a problem, and soon your problem starts having problems. Isn't that right?

Second, notice to whom Elijah then goes. God directed the prophet to the little town of Zarephath . . . to one of the poorest women in that town . . . and when he arrived, he found her gathering sticks to build a fire so she could cook the last bit of flour and oil she had into a pancake for herself and her son. She was getting ready to fix her last meal, then give up and die.

Elijah asked her to give him the first portion. He told her that if she gave, she was to expect to receive food back from God, not just a pancake, but enough daily until the rains came—no matter how long that would take. Elijah didn't ask her to give without promising her, under the inspiration of the Holy Spirit, that she was going to get something back. He said, "Bring a little cake to me first, and the Lord says that the meal in your barrel will not diminish and your oil will not decrease until He sends rain again on the earth."

At first the woman couldn't grasp what God was saying to her through His servant, Elijah. To give, then expect to get more back, was beyond her thinking. It took a revelation from the Lord for her to see it. And your logical thinking mind can't see SEED-FAITH until God reveals it to you spiritually—and then you believe Him and take a step of faith.

Friend, the *receiving* part—getting something back from God—is attached to the *giving* part. They are divinely linked together. One doesn't happen without the other.

What does this mean to your life today?

It means that God can make a way for you to *receive* even when it seems there is no way, if you give first.

It means that your ability to receive is directly linked to your giving. Receiving *follows* giving. It is as automatic as breathing in and breathing out. You need to expect to *receive* . . . to get what God has promised back to you in His Word.

Well, Dr. Sackett read 1 Kings 17 carefully, and soon he returned to me and handed me a hundred-dollar bill.

I said, "Will you expect God to multiply it back to you on the basis of the Word of God?"

"I will."

Now you can't always tell if a person means it when he says, "I will." You have to wait and see what happens.

This happened in my Baltimore, Maryland, Crusade that ran for sixteen days.

The day after Dr. Sackett gave me the hundred-dollar bill, he came to me and handed me several bills.

"What's this?" I asked.

He said, "A man I've never met before in my life came up to me and handed me this three hundred dollars."

"Great!" I said. "But why are you giving it to me?"

"I want to put this in as a seed, too. I want to see how God will multiply it back!"

I said, "I'll believe with you."

A few more days went by, and Dr. Sackett came back again.

He actually looked as if he was ten feet off the ground, the enthusiasm on his face was so great.

"Somebody just gave me *seven* hundred dollars!" he said.

By this time Dr. Sackett was really enjoying himself . . . enjoying what God was doing . . . enjoying the sowing *and* reaping—the giving and receiving—of his SEED-FAITH. "I want to plant this seven hundred, too," he said.

On the last day of the crusade, a woman came up to him out of the audience and said, "Dr. Sackett, I've heard about the work you are doing with Oral Roberts. I want to know if you will accept fourteen hundred dollars from me for the Hebrew Bibles that will go to Israel?"

Dr. Sackett rushed to me and said, "Look what I've received!" And then he went on, "Tomorrow's Monday. I'm going straight to the printer first thing in the morning. I'm going to get the presses rolling for all the Hebrew Bibles this fourteen hundred dollars will pay for."

"Here," I said, "take this other eleven hundred you have given me during these past two weeks. That will make twenty-five hundred dollars as a beginning!"

Dr. Sackett had the Bibles printed, but after we had returned to Tulsa he sought me out. He was in tears. I said, "Why are you crying? Didn't God bless you?"

He said, "Yes, but just think if I had given you the fourteen hundred. Think how God would have multiplied *that*, and I could have sent more Hebrew Bibles to Israel." He felt devastated.

Until the day he died, Dr. Sackett often repeated those words to me, each time with a hurt in his heart. He had discovered that you can never give too much to God . . . and you can never receive too much *back* from God. He learned a great lesson, and so did I. It took us three years, but we did get a hundred thousand Bibles in the Hebrew language. They were then distributed in Israel over several months. You can still find many of them there in the schools and libraries today. And in many ways, I know that seed is being multiplied over . . . and over . . . and over again by God.

But I will never forget how Dr. Sackett, once he got hold of

SEED-FAITH, wept so many times over not planting that fourteen hundred dollars to the Lord. He believed it would not have taken three years but three months to get a hundred thousand Hebrew Bibles into Israel.

"But," you say, "what if I can't really know the best result for me?"

When people say that to me, I always sense that they are afraid of asking for too much. Friend, within the bounds of reason, you can't ask God for too much.

If you need a car . . . ask God for the best car He has for you.

If you need a spouse . . . ask God for the best one He has for you.

If you need a job . . . ask God for the best job He has for you.

If you need a healing . . . ask God for complete healing and the best health He has for you.

"But," you say, "how can I know my seed *will* grow and *will* bear a harvest?"

Because that's the nature of a seed. It's in a seed's nature to grow when the conditions are right. Stop to think about it a moment. A seed can't help growing when it's planted into warm, moist, nutritious soil. That's the way God created a seed.

When you plant into the good soil of God's work, your seed can't *help* growing.

"But," you say, "I don't have a lot to plant. What if my seed isn't good enough?"

No seed is too small.

Recently a student at Oral Roberts University was in chapel where he heard my son Richard tell about his plans for going to Jamaica to hold crusade services. This young man wanted to give to make that trip possible because he could see that it was good soil for seed. Souls were going to be saved, people were going to be healed, lives were going to be changed for the Lord.

He looked in his pockets . . . his wallet . . . and all he found to give were a Cross pen and fifteen cents. He gave them. He gave them expecting God to multiply those seeds and use them for the work in Jamaica. He also expected God to multiply them so that his own personal needs might be met.

Within six weeks, this young man wrote us a letter telling us what had happened. His letter was so full of enthusiasm the words almost jumped off the page. He had received several checks from totally unexpected directions, and they totaled fifteen hundred dollars—a ten-thousandfold increase—much more than enough to cover the present urgent bills that he had been facing. And on top of that, he had received *three* Cross pens from people who didn't know he had given his pen away!

His SEED-FAITH miracle catapulted him—and many more who knew of it—into a dynamic new relationship with Jesus. After several months he's still one excited young man, and we're excited with him . . . and for him.

He has proved again that the seed you have to plant . . . anything you have to give . . . is big enough in God's eyes.

When Jesus saw the widow in the Temple throw her two pennies into the offering box, He commented on how *much* she had given (see Mark 12:41–44). It wasn't the amount of money that caught Jesus' eye. It was the fact that this woman had given out of her lack . . . her need . . . her want. She had given all she had, expecting God to give her all she needed.

Whatever you have to give, wrap it up with your love . . . with your faith . . . with joy . . . with thanksgiving . . . and release it to God's work. Do it expecting God to honor it . . . multiply it . . . and give it back to you in the very form you need the most.

After you've planted your seed—given to God's work—start looking for your harvest. Start expecting something from God to come into your life. When you receive it, I mean when you "get" it, take a portion of it and plant it again. Get into the rhythm of sowing and reaping . . . of giving and receiving . . . just like you are breathing out and breathing in.

You know a farmer doesn't plant one crop and harvest it and then wait until he has need of food before he plants again. No, when he reaps the harvest, he plants immediately again for the next season's crop. In many places in our country, a farmer has several different types of crops at some stage all the time. He's in a continual, continuous process of planting and reaping, planting and reaping.

Continual and continuous is God's plan for your SEED-FAITH. "But," you say, "doesn't this make me greedy, Oral Roberts?"

Not if you're really into SEED-FAITH. If you're into getting and keeping, you can fall into greed. But if you're into giving and receiving, receiving and giving, in a rhythm over and over, you are into *living* by your faith and *growing* in your faith and *using* your faith.

The Bible teaches that we can grow from strength to strength (see Ps. 84:7). What does that mean? It means that as we give and receive, we cause our very lives to be multiplied. We get back even more to give to grow into more to receive . . . and then again even more than that to give and receive. And all the time your faith is growing stronger and becoming more potent, your witness for Christ is more natural to you and more effective, your life is more meaningful, your relationship with Jesus Christ is warmer and richer! You are a happy person no matter how often other needs come. You know you have SEED-FAITH planted against your need.

As you live in the pattern and rhythm of SEED-FAITH, you discover recovery is within the bounds of your experience. In The King James Version, Jesus speaks of recovery as "being made whole" (see for example, John 5:6, 14). Jesus knows that wholeness is a state of being that has to be *made* to happen. You provide the seed, no matter how little or much, and Jesus will be at work to make you whole.

Speaking personally out of experience with SEED-FAITH for these many exciting years, I testify to you that at first it goes against your grain to accept getting something back from the seeds you plant. I've discovered it's easier for me to give than to expect to receive, and I've had to literally believe the Word of God rather than the way I was taught. I encourage you to be more courageous in humbling yourself to expect to get something back lest you end up denying God as a good God and as a Rewarder of each of us who diligently seeks to love Him and put Him first in giving and living.

You have needs now, and you'll have needs tomorrow and

next week and right on until you get to heaven. Take God's SEED-FAITH way. Try it—you'll love the miracles.

As you get into the rhythm of planting your faith seeds, it's important that you accompany them with your FAITH-TALK. Your FAITH-TALK is the way you cultivate your SEED-FAITH.

Consider

1. Are you trusting an employer for your wages or are you trusting God for an *income*, an inflow, that will satisfy all areas of your life?

2. How are you currently giving to God? Are you giving your best? Are you giving out of your need? Are you giving some of the very thing you need back in miracle abundance?

3. Are you giving for a desired result? Are you having difficulty in expecting to receive back from God? Have you been taught that it is wrong to receive back or to give for a desired result? What does the Bible *really* teach?

4. Are you planting your seeds of faith in good soil?

Use Faith-Talk

Let me use this chapter to pull together several thoughts that I've shared with you only briefly in other places in this book.

The first thought is that our faith comes by hearing. The Bible says that "faith comes by hearing, and hearing by the word of God" (Rom. 10:17).

It says faith *comes*. That means that your faith is like oil in the ground. It's there . . . it's to be used and released . . . but you have to drill for it and cause it to *come forth*.

It says faith comes by *hearing*. Most of us think about hearing in relationship to other people. "Did you hear what the preacher said?" "Did you hear what he said . . . or she said . . . about a matter?" But the fact is that you also hear what you yourself say.

And when it comes right down to it, people who have studied the way we learn tell us that we remember only about ten percent of what other people say to us. Only about that much lodges in us and becomes a part of our memories. On the other hand, we remember about ninety percent of what we ourselves have to say!

What does that mean to you and me today? It means that our own words are even more important to our faith than the words we hear from other people. What you say directly affects how you believe!

Finally, that verse says our faith comes by hearing the *Word of*

God. To speak the Word of God, you've got to know the Word of God. You've got to know what the entire Bible says, not just one or two isolated verses here and there. You've got to know more of what the Bible says as a whole. You've got to get the thread of the Bible as God has woven it throughout His Word. Then you will see how God has repeatedly said things and done things. You will see what Jesus said and did as a whole, and you will get the big picture of God's plan and purpose for all of mankind—and for yourself in particular.

That's one of the reasons, by the way, that we are building the Healing Center now in Tulsa. In it we will have a multi-media, three-dimensional "experiential theater" presentation of a great journey through the Bible, depicting some of the outstanding moments of faith from Genesis to Revelation. If you visit Tulsa and see the "Journey through the Bible," you will have an opportunity to see the whole of the Bible . . . to see God's master plan for you and all humanity . . . to experience the way God made the world . . . and to see how God does things so you can better learn how to do things His way.

As I shared with you earlier, I heard God speak to me specifically as I was being carried to the tent meeting where I was prayed for and where I began to receive my healing of tuberculosis. God said, "I am going to heal you, and you are to take my healing power to your generation."

I went for years without knowing exactly what that meant or how to do it. I started preaching almost immediately after I was healed. I pastored small churches in several areas as I struggled to know *how* to take God's healing power to this generation.

I didn't have any role models. I didn't know how to pray for the sick. I didn't know all that I know today about the ways in which God heals people. The best I knew to do was to go to my Bible and fast and pray and ask God what to do.

For several nights I dreamed the same dream. In it I saw people the way God sees people—the teeming masses going through life with hurting, gaping wounds, everybody sick in some way. Some were sick in their bodies, others in their souls, some in their emotions, many in their relationships and in their finances. Everybody had a need. *Everybody*.

*Are you
speaking poor-talk?
Sick-talk?
Down-in-the-dumps
defeated talk?
Replace it with*
FAITH-TALK.

*Your spirit
is listening
all the time
to what
you are speaking
with your mouth.
Are you
encouraging
yourself?*

Evelyn would awaken to find me weeping somewhere in our little house. I would unknowingly get out of bed and wander through the house until the weight of that dream forced me to my knees.

I was also forced to my knees in another way. That was in prayer. I began to fast and pray and ask God to show me, show *me*, SHOW ME how to heal people as Jesus did. I read the four Gospels and the book of Acts through again and again—three times in a period of thirty days while on my knees. And as I prayed and fasted and read, I began to see Jesus rise up from the pages. I saw that He was always in motion. I saw that He was always reaching out to people and healing them. He was on His way to heal someone, coming from someplace where He had just healed someone, or He was in the very act of healing someone. The words of Jesus rang in my ears.

I also heard God speak again, "Don't be like other men. Be like *Jesus*."

Friend, there's no role model for you anywhere on this earth like Jesus. Jesus became real to me as never before. And let me tell you, when Jesus becomes real to you, there is no person you'll ever meet so appealing. When Jesus becomes real to you, you find yourself attracted to Him. You want to know Him more . . . be more like Him . . . and do the things He did. You want to talk the way He talked, and Jesus used FAITH-TALK.

What exactly is FAITH-TALK?

It's almost easier to describe what *isn't* FAITH-TALK. FAITH-TALK is the opposite of sick-talk, or poor-talk, of doubt-talk, or of negative down-in-the dumps talk.

You say, "What do you mean?"

You've heard sick-talk . . .

"Oh, I just don't think I can do that today. My bursitis is acting up. And my head hurts."

You've heard poor-talk . . .

"We just can't afford that. Times are tough. We have to be careful with what we give to God."

You've heard doubt-talk . . .

"Well, I'm just not sure that'll work. It's kind of risky to try . . ."

You've heard negative down-in-the-dumps talk . .

"Things just aren't going so well right now . . ."

Now hear the flip side of those same records.

FAITH-TALK:

"I'm going to get out of bed this morning and do everything I can to turn this bad situation around."

FAITH-TALK:

"I'm going to give this to God and trust Him to multiply it into the harvest of miracles I need."

FAITH-TALK:

"Let's give it a try. I'll do my best to make it happen."

FAITH-TALK:

"We're on the verge of winning. We're about to have a breakthrough."

One night Jesus decided that it was time to go to Gadara to command the demons to leave a man who was dwelling outside the city, a man who was beside himself, unable to take control over his thoughts and actions. Jesus said to His disciples, "Let us get in this boat and cross over the Sea of Galilee."

They did as Jesus said, and as soon as they were on board, Jesus went into the back of the boat and fell asleep. He knew He was going to wake up in Gadara.

A storm struck, however, before they arrived. Storms can come up very quickly on the Sea of Galilee. The winds come whipping down the mountains that surround the lake, and within a matter of minutes, the entire lake can be churning with whitecaps.

The disciples were in terror. Storms like this could capsize a boat in seconds. They rushed to awaken Jesus. They cried, "Don't you care what is happening? How can you sleep through this? We're about to go under!"

Jesus responded to them this way: "Where is your faith?" In other words, "What are *you* doing about it? Why aren't you using your faith to come against this problem? Why aren't *you* speaking to the winds and the waves to settle down?"

Then Jesus rose up, and He spoke, "Peace, be still! Stop your ranting and raving. That's enough. Peace, be *still!*"

And the winds and the waves obeyed His voice, and the Bible says, "They came to the other side of the sea." (See Mark 4:35–5:1.)

I want you to see three things here. First, Jesus spoke. There is power in spoken words.

Second, Jesus spoke against the problem. The Bible says He *rebuked* the wind. He said, "Stop it. That's enough."

And finally, Jesus spoke for the result He wanted. He said, *"Peace, be still now."*

That's a good model for you to use. Address your problem with your words. Get it out. Speak it out. Don't let your problem ferment inside you.

Speak against it. Tell it to go.

Jesus told His disciples later, "If you *say* to this mountain, 'Be removed and be cast into the sea, it *will* be done'" (Matt. 21:21, italics added). Address your problem, and command it to leave.

And then speak out the result you want to have. Voice it. Don't just think it. *Say* it.

Your attitude . . . your ideas . . . your faith are all going to feed on what you say. If you say the right words, you're going to start believing the right things. When you believe the right things, you can act in the right way.

Now you may ask, "How do I know what to say?"

Say what your Bible says.

"But," you say, "how do I know what the Bible says?"

Read it. Study it. Hear it in church. Listen to it on tape from those who have recorded it for you to hear. Get the Word of

God into you. Memorize it. Speak it to yourself. Speak it to others.

Finally, make it a habit to listen more closely to what you are saying. Are you talking poor-talk? *Stop it.* Are you talking sick-talk? *Stop it.* Are you talking doubt-talk? *Stop it.*

Pay attention when you open your mouth. Do it consciously. If you don't do it consciously, I can guarantee you that you will still be listening to yourself with your spirit.

For years, I opened our television broadcasts with this phrase: "Something *good* is going to happen to you." Friend, that's FAITH-TALK.

Millions of people around the world know my phrase, "Expect a miracle!" Friend, that's FAITH-TALK.

I've preached that "you can't go under for going over." Friend, that's FAITH-TALK.

How does your FAITH-TALK work with SEED-FAITH? It reminds you that you've planted a seed and that you're in a state of expectancy. FAITH-TALK says, "I'm a *giving* person, and I'm expecting to be a *receiving* person. I'm God's person, and I'm in God's rhythm of sowing and reaping, giving and receiving, planting and harvesting."

FAITH-TALK reminds you that you have a miracle on the way.
FAITH-TALK waters the seeds you've sown.

FAITH-TALK encourages those around you. It creates a climate of faith.

Now let me tell you two more things about FAITH-TALK so that you can see it as a whole.

First, FAITH-TALK is not presumption. It's not pie-in-the-sky wishful thinking. FAITH-TALK has to be based on God's Word and on what God desires for you in this life. The Bible says, "Faith is the substance of things hoped for, the evidence of things not seen" (Heb. 11:1). You've got to have evidence for your faith. You can't just go about saying whatever comes into your mind and call that FAITH-TALK. FAITH-TALK is speaking the words of Jesus to your situation. It's saying what Jesus would say if Jesus were present in a physical way to say the words.

That's why you've got to know as much as you can of what's

in your Bible. This will help you to *know* what Jesus would say.

Second, FAITH-TALK has two relatives: love-talk and hope-talk. It's balanced by our love and hope. We can't use our FAITH-TALK to build up something for ourselves if it means that someone else is going to lose in the process.

Let me give you an example. Let's say you want a better job. You want to do something that is better suited to your skills and that brings you more reward and gives you more meaning in your life. You begin to plant your seeds of faith for that desired result. And along the way, you use your FAITH-TALK: "I'm going to get that promotion. I'm going to get a better job. Jesus said He wants me to prosper. He wants me to do more with my talents."

That's FAITH-TALK.

It is *not* FAITH-TALK to say, "I'm going to have my boss's job. He's going to get fired. He's going to get in trouble and be forced to leave. I'm going to get his position."

No, that's just some sort of blabbering to try to convince yourself of something. FAITH-TALK operates out of love for others *and* love for yourself. It operates for the good of all. In God's plans, everybody wins except the devil and his crowd.

FAITH-TALK builds the same way SEED-FAITH builds. The more you use your FAITH-TALK, the more you'll find yourself talking FAITH-TALK. The more people will enjoy being around you to hear what you have to say. And . . . the more you'll enjoy listening to yourself!

FAITH-TALK also opens up your mind to the methods that God wants to use to bring you the miracles you need.

How?

Well, have you ever heard yourself say something and then stop and ask yourself, "Did *I* say that?" This happens to me many times when I am preaching. I will say something that I really know is "hot off the wire."

You may find yourself speaking out the very solution that God has for your problem.

But there's something else that also happens. When you begin to speak out with your FAITH-TALK, others feel more free to use *their* FAITH-TALK. You may find others speaking to you under the moving of the Holy Spirit, inspiring you to try something that you hadn't thought of or to call someone you hadn't called or to look for something you hadn't even known existed.

You may find yourself talking about a method or an instrument that you hadn't considered! It may be the very method that God your Source is going to use to bring you the miracles you need!

And that's the next signpost on your road to recovery. . . .

Consider

1. What kinds of messages are you speaking to your own spirit? Do you talk more about problems or solutions? Needs or answers? Defeat or victory in Jesus Christ?

2. Have you commanded your problem to leave? Have you spoken out the result you want? Does your result match up with what the Bible teaches that God wants you to have?

3. What are some examples you have heard of "sick talk," "poor talk," or "doubt talk"? What would be the FAITH-TALK opposite?

4. What can you say today to build up someone you know—to express hope and love to that person?

Take Advantage of All God's Methods

I first met Jim Winslow at a Titan basketball game at Oral Roberts University in the late 1960s. Today he is our chief executive officer of the City of Faith Health-Care Center and the head of our medical education program at Oral Roberts University. Back then he was a well-respected orthopedic surgeon in our community and a man our coaches turned to when one of their players got hurt.

I really got to know Jim, though, when he came to me one day in extreme discouragement.

Jim had been in an accident that had severely injured his right hand. The ends of his fingers had been partially severed, and he had lost all feeling in them. His fellow surgeons had done everything they knew to put the nerve endings back together, but several weeks had passed since the surgery and Jim still had no sensation in the tips of his right fingers.

He called and asked if he could see me. I invited him to our home, and when he arrived, he held out his right hand. "See those fingers?" he said.

I looked at them. They were rough and red. "What happened?"

His six-foot four-inch body shook as he told me his story. As an orthopedic surgeon, he had put the limbs of thousands of people back together, including many who had been horribly mutilated in automobile and industrial accidents. Now Jim had been injured himself and in a way that threatened his entire career.

He concluded his story with these words, "Oral, I'll never operate again unless God heals me. Without feeling in these fingers of my operating hand, my career is over. I'll have to give up my practice. Surgery is my career. It is the way I feed my family and clothe them and educate my children. It is also my *life*. God has called me to be a surgeon. It's what I love to do."

Then he asked, "Will you pray for my fingers?"

By this time there were tears in our eyes.

I said, "I'm going to lightly brush my fingers across yours, Jim. Try not to think of my hand doing this, but try to visualize Jesus' hand touching your fingers, You know Jesus as the Great Physician can do what no man can do."

We bowed our heads, and I said, "Jesus, You are closer to us than our breath. You sat where Jim sits, You felt what he feels. The stripes on Your back are for Jim's healing. Jesus, You know the seeds of faith Jim has sown. Heal him, Jesus, heal him."

There was no sudden change in Jim's condition. He thanked me for praying and left. Later he told me, "As I left your house, a quietness came over my spirit. A *knowing* entered me that I was going to be all right."

Weeks passed before I saw Jim again. Then I heard through friends that he was performing surgery again.

Jim came over to me at a basketball game and showed me his fingers. "All the feeling isn't back *yet*," he said, "but there's enough feeling to operate. I'm okay!"

Several years later I found myself in a position where I needed to go to Jim. And how grateful I was for his healing!

It happened during the last meeting of a great crusade—a meeting that, by human reasoning, I should have never held. I had been away the week before, holding a crusade where I had preached and then touched and prayed for around seven thousand sick people in *one day* alone. Many had received healing help from the Lord. But the healing power going through me had so exhausted me that at the close of the services I had to have help just to get in the car. At the close of the meeting, I

*Don't close
your mind
to the*
miracle method
*God may have
for you.*

Don't limit God!

scarcely woke up for three days and nights, and when I did, I hardly knew where I was. I had just barely regained my strength when I started the next series of meetings.

Now it was the last service of my second crusade in two weeks. I had personally prayed for nearly ten thousand people during the week. I had moved into the invalid room to begin the healing service for the final time, and I was lifting an invalid into my arms to pray for him. Compassion was flowing through me for this man . . . my faith was working . . . I felt as strong as five men . . . but when I stood up after praying, something snapped in my left shoulder.

I didn't stop. I couldn't. There were still several thousand people waiting outside in the main hall for prayer. In pain and in an extremely exhausted state, I continued my work.

The next day I awoke feeling tired but wanting some sunshine and fresh air. I decided to go down to the golf course to play a few holes. Golf has been one of the greatest things in my life for helping me keep physically fit. As I swung the first club, my left shoulder snapped again. Play ended in pain on the first hole that day.

As soon as I got back to Tulsa, I called Jim. He examined me and discovered that I had injured the rotator cuff in my left shoulder. The "rotator cuff" is the part of the shoulder that allows the shoulder bones to move. Jim prayed for me and then scheduled surgery for me. He said, "If you're healed directly by God before then, we'll cancel. But if not, then I know God wants to use me in surgery to get you well."

In the days before surgery was scheduled, I got all the prayer I could get. I received some relief but not a complete healing. Since I've always believed strongly in medical science, I decided to go ahead with surgery.

A friend asked me, "Won't you be embarrassed for people to know *you* are having surgery?"

"Why?" I asked.

"Well, won't it weaken their faith that God heals?"

"Why?" I asked again. "Are you saying God heals only through prayer?"

"Well, you are best known for your prayers for the sick."

"Yes, I am. But God should be known for healing people through prayer or surgery or in many other ways. God should get the glory no matter *how* the person is healed. God is the *Healer*. If I come through this surgery with my shoulder healed, I'll thank Dr. Winslow and pay the surgical fee, but I'll know *God did the healing*."

"But, I thought . . ."

"Listen," I said, "I'm not intimidated by people who say they don't believe in miraculous healing through prayer. I know what I've seen and experienced. I've seen thousands of miracles done by God through the power of prayer. I've seen them at close range—within the length of my own arm and hand.

"But neither am I going to be intimidated by people who say they don't believe in medical healing," I said. "I go right ahead and get all the medical help I can get. God has healed me both ways—through medicine and surgery and through prayer. The most powerful help I've received has actually been when I had both working at the same time. And I expect healing at all times through whatever means God chooses."

I believe it is critically important that we not stop the flow of God's healing power into our lives—into our spirits, emotions, minds, finances, relationships, as well as our physical bodies. God has many methods of healing.

Prayer and medicine are only two of the more obvious, well-known methods. God can use a change in climate to bring healing to a person's life . . . or a change in the amount of exercise a person gets. I'm for all of God's methods. God is the Source. All other avenues are instruments that are available to Him.

We can shut off one of God's healing streams toward us by not believing that it is valid, by saying, "I don't believe God can work that way." Really, that's an attempt to force God's hand—to dictate to God Himself just how *you* choose for Him to heal you. It's presumptuous to assume that you even *know* God's best method in your life. It's also foolish to close off anything that can bring healing into your life.

Jim performed the surgery on my shoulder, and the Tulsa news media announced my hospitalization. I was glad. I felt that many would pray for me when they heard about it, and they did. Several of my minister friends came by and prayed while I was still under the anesthetic. (The City of Faith was not built at that time.)

When I was fully conscious, a hospital chaplain came to see me. I waited for his prayer. Instead, he asked me to pray for him.

There I was, my left shoulder tightly bandaged, and the chaplain asked me to pray for *him!* Well, I asked him to lean over so I could touch him and pray. A powerful energy moved through me into him. He was helped with the problem he had. He went out of my room rejoicing and praising God. And immediately I remembered the principle of God that I knew worked in every situation: the principle of sowing in faith and reaping a harvest of miracles. I had just planted a seed of prayer for healing in the life of this minister. Now I was in the best position possible to *expect* healing back into my own shoulder. The Bible teaches in James 5:16 that we are to pray one for another, that *we* may be healed. The seed of prayer that we pray for others is multiplied back to us for our own healing and blessing.

I learned a great lesson as I recovered from my shoulder surgery. Actually, it was a lesson I had first learned many years ago after my healing and recovery from tuberculosis.

On the night that I had received prayer—back there in the tent where the evangelist had prayed for me as my mother and father held me up—I had received an *instant burst* of healing in my lungs.

You say, "Oral Roberts, it all happened in just a moment of time?"

No, it didn't. But it started in a moment of time. The hemorrhaging dried up immediately, and my lungs opened so I could breathe all the way down. None of that was visible, but I knew within myself that health was bursting loose throughout my being from my feet to my head.

It's right here that I've seen some people make some very serious mistakes . . . or some very wonderful decisions. Some people have it in their heads that a person being healed has to show some unmistakable outward sign immediately.

Otherwise they assume that nothing is happening. That's a mistake made about both prayer and medical help. People think that if a person prays—or starts taking proper medication—and they don't see something dramatic happen in an instant, then nothing is happening. I've learned that's a wrong way to think.

I've prayed for some people, and there was no visible sign that indicated they were being healed. And yet they let me know weeks or months later that something *had* happened and *was still happening* to restore them to health and wholeness. Other people seemed to be helped immediately, but they don't go on to get much more healing after that.

Don't get me wrong. I've seen healing that started out quickly and turned out to be complete and lasting. I've seen some healings start out slowly, and very little happens after that. And I've seen some prayers I've prayed that didn't seem to have any effect at all.

Every healing has its own length of time. Some are quick. Some are slow. Some don't even appear to happen in this lifetime but will happen through the resurrection power of Jesus after death. (God always heals His own, even if it takes the resurrection!)

Every healing starts in an instant. It may be a split second when the chemicals of your body finally begin to react properly . . . or when you've finally rearranged the substances of your body through the right diet . . . or when you've finally balanced your checkbook . . . or when you've finally had that breakthrough in communication with a relative or friend . . . or when your attitude and your body come together in a positive, dynamic way . . . or when healing prayer collides with full force into your faith so that something positive literally explodes inside your spirit.

When that instant comes for your healing to start, you have

to seize it. You have to grab it and hold on. You have to believe that it's happening with every part of your being.

If you don't grab hold and hang on to your *moment of healing*, you'll likely lose it. I almost did.

Did you know that you can lose a healing? That you can squelch it after it bursts forth? That you can have a reversal on your road to recovery?

You can.

Following the start of my healing that night, we all got back in the car and drove home. It sure was nice not to have to lie down on the mattress in the back. I could sit up and share in the conversation about the good thing that had begun in me.

It never occurred to me that I might have a relapse. It never dawned on me that the feeling of that sudden burst that had flooded through me might go away.

That didn't mean that I had not truly experienced the start of my healing. I had. It was the most thrilling moment of my life to that point. It was real. But in all of my good feeling, I had just assumed that the bursting-forth moment of my healing would go on and on.

Now you may not feel a bursting-forth time like I did. You may say, "Oral Roberts, I'm apparently a quieter person than you are. My feelings don't run as deep as yours. Things happen to me more gently. Suppose I don't feel health bursting through me like you did?"

Well, first, I accept you as you are because I believe God does. If you're one of those slow-fused persons, so be it.

Second, even if the burst of health is so small that you can't feel it, let me assure you that it *does* take place and you're to look for it to take place and grow. It's like a seed.

I've gone to the science department at Oral Roberts University, and through a microscope I've seen a seed crack open. I'm absolutely convinced that there is a bursting-forth moment for a seed to change its nature so it can become a plant, grow, and produce fruit. It's a principle, a fundamental basic law of God. It's true for all areas of life.

But once that seed begins to grow, it needs to be nutured . . . .

cultivated . . . tended. A healing is more than a bursting-forth moment. It's a process. And again let me point out that it's a process that involves your entire life . . . with many methods . . . but God remains the Source.

Let me tell you what happened in my life. During the next several days after the healing meeting, I was almost like any other person. I began to act well. I didn't have those awful spells of coughing. I didn't experience the nightly bed sweats or the bleeding from my lungs. My appetite returned. The disease of tuberculosis was gone from my body, but I was far from being a whole person.

You say, "Oral Roberts, what do you mean?"

I'm saying that God sees you as a *whole*. You may think your problem is some disease . . . or just a problem in one relationship . . . or just a financial problem. That's not the entire truth of the matter. Whatever the *main* problem appears to be, it becomes a problem in *every* area of your life in one way or another. And you don't solve the entire problem when you solve just one part of it.

In my life, my *body* had experienced an instant burst of healing. But my attitude was still sick. I was still thinking and feeling and believing like a *sick* person. I, myself, Oral Roberts, the entire person, had not been "made whole."

How did Jesus heal people?

He said, "Thou art made *whole*," or, "Thy faith hath made thee whole" (John 5:14, Luke 17:19, King James Version; italic's added). God deals in whole-person healing, not just problem solving.

Note specifically that Jesus often said "*made* whole." Whole-person healing is both a beginning act and an ongoing *making*, a process that never stops.

If you squelch the bursting-forth period, your healing will never come. But it's equally true that if you squelch the ongoing process, you will never be *made whole*.

At one point in my life, I thought of sickness as an *eye* being injured or a *heart* being damaged or *lungs* having a sickness.

I've often heard doctors and nurses make statements about "the eye in Room 224" or "the heart in Room 294."

At first I didn't know what they meant. Later I learned that they had just fallen into the bad habit of *not* saying, "I have a patient in this room with a bad eye"—or foot or heart or whatever the problem was. I don't like to hear patients referred to in that way. God didn't create us as a foot plus a heart plus an eye and so forth. He created us as human beings—with spirit, mind, body, emotions, relationships, spiritual and material needs. (Read 1 Cor. 12:12-20.)

You've got a body . . . but you're more than physical.

You've got a mind . . . but you're more than mental.

You've got emotions . . . but you're more than emotional.

You are a spiritual being who has a body, a mind, a set of emotions, an attitude, and material goods. God sees you as a *whole*.

The one thing we're really trying to do at the City of Faith Health-Care Center is to see people as *whole* men and women. You've got to see yourself as a *whole*, too, so you can really understand this: No matter what's wrong with you . . . it's part of a whole. God wants you whole with every part of your life working in harmony.

You have to go after wholeness. It doesn't just happen automatically. It must be made to happen.

After a few days of feeling on top of the world, I noticed that the shine of my healing experience began to rub off. My strength began to ebb. The burst of health seemed to get weaker and weaker. Doubts began to set it. I couldn't understand why the great strength I had felt in that first hour of my healing didn't continue.

My mother found me sitting with my back against the side of the house one afternoon, and she had a little talk with me. She said, "Oral, you think you weren't really healed, don't you?"

"Well, Mama," I said, "why do I still feel so weak? Why don't I feel the way I did that night—strong enough to do anything?"

She said, "Oral, you've been sick a long time. You've been in bed for more than five months. No doubt the tuberculosis had taken root in you long before they brought you home. Now God has begun to heal you. You're on the right path to getting well. But you've got to remember a couple of things."

"Like what, Mama?"

"Well, do you remember how you felt when you received the healing prayer?"

"I do remember, Mama. I can't ever forget it."

"Every time you feel weak in your body, let your mind go back to the power of God opening your lungs. Oral, God touched you instantly. But it will take weeks, maybe months for you to recover fully and get all your strength back. Don't forget in the five months you were in bed, you lost your strength even to walk. We'll have you start doing some light work so you'll get stronger."

It was hard for me to understand. "Well, Mama, why do I have to lie down some during the day? Why don't I have enough strength to stay up all day?"

My wise little mother looked me in the eye and said, "Oral, it's all right to lie down an hour or two a day for a while. But don't take off your clothes and put on your pajamas. Just lie across the bed with your clothes on."

"What good will that do?" I asked.

"Oral, if you undress, put on your pajamas, and get under the covers, the whole image of your five months in bed with tuberculosis will come back into your mind. But if you lie across the covers fully dressed, you'll think you're only resting to help get your strength back. Do it like I tell you and you'll recover. You'll be learning a new attitude."

Then she said, "Oral, you are *still* operating in faith to make your healing *continue* to happen."

My mother, as I told you, was part Indian. And when Mama had said all she came to say, she abruptly turned and walked away. That was it. I could take it or leave it. She had come to help me. But she couldn't make me do it, and she wouldn't make me do it. She had told me how to get into an attitude of health receiving, of *full* recovery, of *wholeness, but the bottom line was that I was going to have to make it happen.*

I did what Mama had said . . . literally. I took naps and rested. But I never crawled back into bed in the middle of the day. I remembered the moment of bursting forth of my healing every time I became discouraged. Mama continued to encourage me. Within twelve months, I had my weight and strength back, and I had preached my first little sermon! Those twelve months did something to help all of me to be made whole, not just my lungs. My healing was both an act and a process.

You may think that you are just going through a divorce. But chances are that your marriage was sick for quite some time before the divorce took place. Something happened to more than just your marriage relationship, friend. Something happened to *you* during that time. All of you. You need a whole-person healing. It's going to take a process of recovery. You are going to have to make it happen.

You may think that you are just going through a financial problem. But your finances spill over to the way you feel in your body and the way you relate to other people. Something is happening to your *life.* You need a whole-person healing. It's going to take a process of recovery. You are going to have to make it happen.

You may think that you are just going through surgery. But your body is going to have to mend, and that is going to take time. Your attitude . . . your loved ones . . . your finances are all woven into your regaining your full health. You need a whole-person healing. It's going to take a process of recovery. You are going to have to make it happen.

Be thou *made* whole!

Years later, I knew I was up against the need for a whole-person *process* of healing when Jim walked into my bedroom at home one evening and hung a rope from the ceiling so that it hung close to the wall.

"What's that for?" I asked him.

He said, "That, my friend, is an exercise device to help you raise your left hand and arm until you get full motion back."

I asked simply, "You mean the surgery on my shoulder wasn't enough?"

He said, "Oral, you have prayed for enough sick people to know the act of healing is only the beginning. Right?"

"Right."

Jim said, "The best results my patients have ever experienced occurred because of what they did after surgery. Also the worst results."

"Explain."

"I have one man whose shoulder is still stiff after five years. He literally refused to do the exercises he needed to do. Then there is a woman who had knee surgery. I've done that operation on hundreds of people with good results. But she flat out refused to use her knee in exercises and walking. Today she still hobbles."

"Okay," I said, "tell me exactly what to do and I'll do it."

He said, "Oral, remember the old saying, 'No pain, no gain.' I want you to stand by the wall and try to run the fingers of your left hand up the wall. When you get your fingers high enough to take hold of the rope, reach over and grab the rope and start pulling your arm and shoulder up. It will hurt, and I mean *hurt.*"

"But will it help me get the full use of my shoulder?"

"Yes."

"And if I don't do it?"

"Your shoulder will be just about as bad as before the surgery."

Jim was right. It hurt. I don't consider myself to be a crybaby, but the first time I inched the fingers of my left hand up the wall, the pain brought tears to my eyes. Then when I pulled the rope and pulled my arm and shoulder up, I couldn't keep the tears from rolling down my face.

Jim walked in one day and saw me. I had my arm extended as high and as straight as I ever did, but my face was wet with tears. He began to laugh.

"What's so funny?" I asked.

"Oh, nothing. I'm laughing because I've found the best patient I've had in many months."

"You mean because I'm experiencing all this pain?"

"No. You're the best patient because you've got an attitude that you're going to get full use of your shoulder!"

I did get the full use of my shoulder back, and I still have it today.

Listen, friend, a healing must *become* health. A start toward recovery must *arrive* at wholeness.

Along the way, you need to get all the help you can get. Don't turn off any of God's methods that are coming toward you. Don't thwart God's healing power as it comes to you. Seize your bursting forth moment of healing. Then cling to it. Get into wholeness—a recovery that permeates every area of your life.

Consider

1. Have you pitted all of God's methods against your problem? Are you getting the best medical help possible? The best prayer help? The best professional advice?

2. What are you doing to turn an *instant burst* of healing into a full recovery?

3. How does your problem affect your total being? Can you see what Jesus means when He says, "Be thou made *whole*"?

4. What process of healing lies in front of you? Can you define it? Describe it?

Plant a Seed of Equal Benefit

On February 11, 1977, Evelyn and I faced the worst struggle our family had ever experienced.

The night before, a plane exploded over a Kansas wheat field in the middle of a severe thunderstorm. Our daughter Rebecca and her husband Marshall were killed instantly.

The next morning, Evelyn opened our door to find my long-time associate Collins Steele standing there with a policeman. She called to me, "Oral! Oral! Will you come in here right now?"

The sound of her voice made me drop everything and hurry to the door. Evelyn was in a state of shock. She tried to tell me what they had told her, but she couldn't get through it. Finally, the policeman said, "Mr. Roberts, I've come to tell you that your daughter and son-in-law are dead."

"What happened?"

Collins told me about the plane crash the night before and then handed me the morning newspaper. The headline across the front page screamed the words: ORAL ROBERTS' DAUGHTER KILLED. It went on to tell of Marshall and Rebecca and the other two couples that were killed.

I can't tell you the grief, the anguish that swept over Evelyn and me. We grabbed each other and held each other tightly. We didn't know what to do.

Then Evelyn said, "Honey, we've got to hurry and get

dressed and go over to Rebecca's house and tell the children before they hear any other way."

I thought of Brenda, then thirteen; Marcia, who was eight; and little John Oral, only five years old. They were waiting at their house with a babysitter for their parents to return home. We dressed as quickly as we could. I thought the hurting in our souls would kill us.

Rebecca, my oldest. The only one of our four children born at home. I had been there when our little curly-haired daughter came out of her mother's body. I held her in my arms just moments after her birth.

Scenes from her life rushed through my mind. Those years of raising her, seeing her married, enjoying the birth and growth of her three precious children—our first grandchild was her daughter Brenda. I remembered the first time Rebecca and Marshall met—when Rebecca was just four years old. Now they had died together. They had gone away for just a few days, and now they would be away for the rest of our lives on the earth.

Only a few weeks before, I had told my partners and people across America to expect a "Breakthrough from Heaven in '77." God had spoken those words in my heart. I believed them. I was looking to God for great and mighty things. Now, only a few weeks into the year, the greatest tragedy of my life had struck with a pain and fury I had never known. It seemed the devil was mocking me: "Where is your breakthrough from heaven? You've preached that God is a good God. Now what do you have to say?"

Another of my longtime associates, Ron Smith, had arrived by the time Evelyn and I were ready to leave the house, and he offered to drive us over to Marshall and Rebecca's home where the children were. On the way I said aloud, "God, You know something about this that we don't know."

Over and over I said it as Evelyn held my hand and Ron drove, the tears filling his eyes, too. "God, You know something about this that we don't know."

It was Saturday morning, and the children usually slept late.

*Are you suffering
from a tragedy
that has struck
without warning
and seemingly
without cause?*

*Plant a seed of
equal benefit.
God can
blot out
your loss
with a
miracle harvest.*

Today, however, they were eating breakfast when we arrived at about seven o'clock. "Why are you up so early?" I said.

Little Marcia said, "We're waiting for Mommy and Daddy. They're coming home today."

And I had to say, "Your mommy and daddy aren't coming home. You'll have to see them in heaven."

Evelyn and I couldn't help it. We burst into tears. Brenda picked up a new plaque I had prepared for my partners. It said, "God is Greater than Any Problem I Have." She clutched it to her breast as the tears flowed. The five of us wrapped our arms around one another and cried and cried. Our daughter, our son-in-law; their mother, their father.

The bodies strewn over the ground, scarcely recognizable. The children suddenly orphaned.

In that moment we didn't think of anybody else's children dying in accidents. We didn't think about others having lost loved ones. We didn't think about other children being orphaned. We only thought of *our* hurt, *our* loss.

Why?

Why?

Why?

Why?

Isn't that the question we always ask when tragedy strikes. Why did this happen to *me*? To *us*? To our family? To our business? To my job? To my marriage?

I readily admit to you that I don't know *why*. There is no easy answer to *why* tragedies strike the way they do. Only God really knows why. Yes, *God knows something about this that we don't know.*

The better question is the one that usually comes hot on the heels of "why?" It's the question, How do I get through this?

First, we faced the future of the children. We knew that Marshall and Rebecca had been very close to Bill and Edna Earle Nash, Marshall's brother and sister-in-law. There had been an agreement between them that if anything ever happened to Marshall and Rebecca, Bill and Edna would take their children. Bill was only two years older than Marshall, but his daughter had been attending Oral Roberts University where Bill was on the board of regents. She had married an ORU graduate and they had moved into their own home. Bill and Edna called us from the St. Louis airport. They had heard the news and were on their way home. Bill said, "We'll raise them like our very own."

Then we met with Reverend and Mrs. Walter Nash, Marshall's parents. We found them strong in the Lord, even though this was the second son they had lost within a period of two years. They, too, agreed that Bill and Edna should have custody of the children. By nightfall, Bill and Edna had returned to Tulsa and had taken the children to their home.

Somehow we made it through that first day.

Soon the Abundant Life Prayer Group was swamped with telephone calls. Love was flowing into our hearts from our dear partners. Telegrams were pouring in to us, many from people we didn't know and many from others like Billy Graham, Dale Evans, President Carter, and others we had met. Our other children stood with us, their grief almost overwhelming, but together we stood as a close family in Christ.

But on the fourth night as Evelyn and I were getting ready for bed, she said, "Oh, Oral, I'm not going to make it tonight. This is the worst night of all."

I knew what she meant. In the midst of all the arrangements that had to be made, the thoughts kept coming, *Was God real after all? Was He good?* I had preached it for thirty years in every state and more than seventy nations. But was God *there?*

Then Evelyn said, "Honey, would you take me in your arms and pray for me?"

I took Evelyn in my arms that night and prayed. She prayed also. And as we prayed, the Holy Spirit flowed through me and I began to know in my spirit God's words back to us in our loss. The first words that I spoke after we prayed were the words of a passage in the Bible:

For we do not wrestle against flesh and blood, but against principalities, against powers, against the rulers of the darkness of this age. . . . Therefore take up the whole armor of God . . . and having done all, to stand. Stand therefore (Eph. 6:12–14).

These words were greatly comforting to us because they took our minds off the immediate circumstances and shifted them onto the meaning behind the circumstances—that we human beings are ultimately each one of us, a battlefield for God and the devil. The devil is on one side seeking to destroy us . . . steal from us . . . and kill us and rob us of our eternal souls. God is on the other side seeking to win us . . . bless us . . . give to us . . . and lead us toward eternal life.

Then I found myself speaking these words from the Lord:

"Go on national television in your half-hour program next Sunday morning and, while you feel the hurt and loss, tell the people how you feel and give witness to My power and to the Resurrection."

Evelyn cried, "I can't do it. It's too soon. I'll break down and won't be able to get through it."

I said, the power of the Holy Spirit compelling me, "Darling, then I'll go on by myself. We've got to plant a seed out of our grief. If we don't plant our seed now, we'll never get the miracle we need to get over this hurt, and it will haunt us the rest of our lives."

She said, "Can't we wait a few months?"

I said, "This grief will destroy us. It'll tear us apart. It'll destroy my ministry. Let's not wait until the storm has passed. Let's tell the people how we feel in the middle of the storm and let them see that we have hurts just like theirs."

Then Evelyn said, "I won't let you do it alone. I'll do it with you. I'll plant my seed, too."

The day came for the broadcast. My associates quickly arranged the cameras, and we started—no music, no introduction. Just us.

As Evelyn and I looked at the camera, we suddenly were aware of all those who had also lost loved ones. With tears streaming down our cheeks, we told how we felt when we lost our daughter and son-in-law. There were moments when the words wouldn't come and we fumbled for them. Although a few of our associates and friends were in the small taping studio with us, we felt so alone.

As the minutes went by, I began to feel more and more the upward swell of the Holy Spirit inside me. It was as if our miracle were already starting to come up out of the seed we were planting out of our need. I heard myself telling how Rebecca and Marshall were real Christians. How they had come to Christ in their youth. How they had lived for Him.

"But," I said, "if they hadn't been Christians, in the brief moments of the plane crash a good God would have given them time to call on His name. And all you who have lost loved ones and don't know if they are saved and are in heaven with our Lord, how do you know there wasn't that moment before their deaths that the Holy Spirit opened their hearts and they accepted Jesus Christ? None of us knows how far God's mercy extends. But we know it extends further than man's."

I added, "On the cross one of the men crucified with Jesus, a thief, had in the last moment cried, 'Lord, remember me when You come into Your kingdom,' and Jesus did."

Then we ended the program with the good news of the Resurrection. By the time the half-hour taping was over, it seemed that heaven had come down and shone across the earth. We could feel it.

When the cameras were turned off, Evelyn and I stood and hugged each other. We had planted our seed of faith. The studio was flooded with love from our associates. God had taken the grief in His great hands and was pulling it out of our hearts.

We said, "We're going to resume our lives. We're going on with this ministry. There is a God. He is good, and He is real to us as never before. He is more real to us through the homegoing of Rebecca and Marshall than we ever could have known. We know they are in heaven, and someday we are going there, too. We believe it."

A few weeks later, Evelyn and I were in the great desert region of the southwestern United States. The area was parched and dry. Then came a thundershower. And almost overnight, the desert began to turn green.

God gave me a promise, "I will rain upon your desert." Soon, the details of the City of Faith Health-Care Center began to unfold before me. Day after day I wrote as fast as I could the words that I felt impressed by God upon my spirit.

By the time we returned to Tulsa, the vision for the City of Faith was clearly spelled out. God had given me new directions for this ministry and for our lives. Out of our greatest tragedy was to emerge one of the greatest victories I've ever experienced in the ministry—the building of the City of Faith!

We had planted a seed of equal benefit, and God was to multiply it into something far greater than our grief.

What has been true of us is true for you:

In every mistake, in every adversity, there is a seed of an equal benefit. If you look for it and plant it, God will multiply it into something greater than the loss you have experienced.

One day I was playing a round of golf with a very important man in our community. I had looked forward to this privilege because I hoped to get a chance witness for the Lord as we played. I got my opportunity—but not in the way I expected.

I stepped up to hit a drive, and I hit a bad one. Now I'm a pretty good golfer when I get to play regularly, but I had not played in a long time. Anyway, I hit the ball, and it wound up under a tree.

My friend made a choice comment, "Too bad, Oral." Then he got serious and said, "Golf is a lot like life. One small mistake and it affects the rest of your life."

I heard myself agreeing with him, but then I stopped. "Wait a minute," I said. "Life is not like golf. If God is your Source . . . and if you are giving as a seed of your faith that you plant, as Christ taught . . . and if you are expecting miracles, then you can turn around any mistakes you make in life."

He said, "What do you mean? Your ball is lying over there under a tree . . ."

I said, "I know I can't replay that stroke. But I'm not out of the game. I've got to go over there under the tree and hit one of the best shots of my life. That's the seed of equal benefit."

He said, "The seed of *what?*"

"Of equal benefit. In every mistake you make in life, God has given you another seed that you can plant. If you plant it with the same faith, then God will multiply it into something greater than the mistake you made."

I went on to share with him a story from the book of Genesis. It was the story of Joseph, one of Jacob's sons. Joseph was Jacob's favorite boy. He was a sensitive child to the things of God, and he had many dreams that were from the Lord. But Joseph told his dreams to his brothers. He even told them that in one of his dreams they had all fallen down and did homage to him.

Their jealousy turned to rage, and one day when Joseph came to them in the fields with a message and provisions from their father, the older brothers plotted to get rid of Joseph. As they were deciding what to do, they spotted a caravan traveling to Egypt, and they decided to sell Joseph into slavery rather than kill him. Thus, Joseph wound up a slave far from home.

But the Bible says that the Lord was with Joseph. Joseph had many temptations in Egypt, but he kept living for the Lord. He served the best he could. He was the best slave he could be.

Again, tragedy overtook him. He was unjustly accused by his master's wife, and he landed in prison. Yet he continued to give, and God blessed him. Finally, he was put in charge of the other prisoners, and in that role, he befriended the king's baker and butler who had lost favor with Pharaoh. Joseph interpreted their dreams.

Later, when the butler was restored to his former position, Pharaoh had a dream that troubled him greatly. None of his wisest counselors could interpret it for him. The butler remembered Joseph and his special ability. And in one day—after years of discouragement, slavery, and hardship—Joseph went from being prisoner to being prime minister of Egypt. His interpretation of a dream in a prison cell had been a seed that reaped a harvest beyond his youthful mistake. In his new position, he was able to provide for his brothers and father in a time of severe famine. The seed Joseph had planted for an equal benefit blotted out the power of the past tragedies of his life.

The Bible has many other stories with similar results. One of my favorites is the story of Job.

Job planted a seed of *prayer* for his friends who were trying to discourage him further in the midst of his trials—the loss of his possessions, his family, his health. Job reaped a harvest of full restoration—two times what he had owned before, fullness of health, and a new family. (See Job 42:8–17.)

There's a lot in the story of Job for you today.

One day the devil said to God, "I don't like this man named Job."

God said, "Why not?"

"He's having it too good. He thinks these things are all that'll come from You. If You take them away and give him some bad deals, You'll see he's not for real. You'll find that he's just pretending to love You and to have a relationship with You."

Do you ever wonder what the devil might be saying to God about your life? Are you a threat to the devil?

Well, it wasn't long before one bad thing after another happened to Job. His children were killed in an accident. His business fell off and finally went under. He became ill in his body and couldn't work anymore. And when he needed his wife the most, she misunderstood and walked out on him. Then his closest friends gathered around to blame him for all that had happened to him and his family. (See Job 1–2.)

I've often said that everybody either has a problem, is a problem, or lives with one. This means that everybody suffers at times.

What's back of it? What causes it?

First, Job suffered as a result of what the devil did to him. I believe there is a real devil. He's *very* real. The Bible talks about the devil as being real. Jesus referred to him as being real. I've experienced enough in my life to know for myself he's real. His job is to oppose any person who tries to live for God.

Second, Job suffered as a result of what men and circumstances did to him. People were envious of Job. A catastrophe took the lives of his children. These things were beyond Job's control. There was nothing he could do to prevent them.

Third, Job suffered as a result of what he did to himself. He said, "For the thing I greatly feared has come upon me, and what I dreaded has happened to me" (Job 3:25).

Every day when I read my mail, people convey the message, "Oral Roberts, I'm so afraid that such and such is going to happen."

Job believed for the worst . . . and he got what he was believing for.

Job's suffering was a combination of what the devil and men and circumstances did to him and what he did to himself by fearing.

Are you in Job's shoes? Wholly or partly? Do you feel deserted and alone? Is the devil really after you? Have you fallen victim to your own mistakes and fears?

What about God? How do you feel toward Him?

Job turned his fear around when he started using his faith. Through it all he clung to God his Source. He said, "Though He slay me, yet will I trust in Him" (Job 13:15).

Things started turning around at that point. And I believe they can turn around in your life, too. Job prayed for his friends who had mistreated him terribly during his loss. He planted that prayer for them as the only seed available to him at the moment. It was his seed for an equal benefit to come to him.

What seeds do you have?

Maybe the seed you have is a seed of prayer. Are you holding something against someone? Are you holding something against God? Can you plant a seed of prayer on behalf of that person or on behalf of yourself?

Maybe the seed you have is a seed of forgiveness. Can you forgive the person who has done you wrong? Can you honestly pray for that person and ask God's best to come into that person's life? That may be the very seed that will overcome the hold that guilt . . . bitterness . . . resentment . . . or anger may have over your life.

Maybe the seed you have is a seed of money. Can you give it?

Can you release it to God's work and trust God to meet your needs?

I have a friend who planted a different kind of seed. He suffered a massive heart attack, and the doctors struggled to keep him alive. Finally, one of them said to the family, "All he's got is a prayer." And the family called me.

I managed to get permission to go into his hospital room, and the family asked me to "take my freedom." Now when you tell me to take my freedom, I'm going to really pray! I got hold of him and began to lay a prayer of faith on him. And then the Spirit gave me an answer to what was the root cause of the problem.

I said to him, "The first thing you've got to do is to make a decision to start paying back what you owe. Even if it's just ten dollars at a time, or twenty, or a hundred. You've got to write some letters or make some phone calls and say, 'I'm sorry, and I'm going to start repaying what I owe you.'"

I knew that his problem was directly related to the bankruptcy proceedings that he was involved in. He owed several million dollars. His family had been breaking up over it. He was trying to escape everything in his life. And yet the worry and guilt and fear had eaten away at him on the inside until his body finally reacted in a way that almost took him out.

He looked up at me from the hospital bed as if to say, "Do you really think that will turn my health around?"

I said, "Listen. We're Christians. We're honest. And sometimes unfortunate things happen. When the bottom drops out, you've got to plant a seed of an equal benefit. You *can* plant another seed. It will wipe out the loss."

"What can I plant? I don't have anything left."

"You have yourself," I said. "Maybe you have never really planted *yourself.*"

"How do I do that?"

I said, "Well, make a decision on this hospital bed that when you put your feet on the floor the next time, you're going to rise up to be God's man. I know you're not a preacher, but you can be God's man without being a preacher. Plant a seed of writing those people you owe. Tell them you've had a failure and you're going to do your best to make it right. And if it means taking the shirt off your back and handing it to them as a symbol, then do it. That's the way to come off the bottom. Then find ways you can start giving of yourself, and I mean you *self*—your ideas, your time, your energy, and, as you have money again, your money."

I didn't see him for some months—it must have been well over a year. And then one day I went down to my favorite hamburger stand. It's a place I can go and be casual in my jeans and my boots. As I went up to the counter, I suddenly felt an arm around my shoulder. It was my friend. He said, "Would you come over and sit with us?"

I said, "Yes." And as we ate together, he told me how he was just on the verge of paying back the last of what he still owed. He had written the letters . . . made the phone calls . . . started giving of himself . . . and he was prospering and paying off his huge debt. He even paid for my hamburger that night!

In the months that followed, he was restored to his family, which meant everything to him.

In the midst of *your* tragedy . . . your loss . . . your devastation . . . *what seed has God placed in your life that you can plant?*

Plant it today. Make a decision that you *will* reap a harvest in return in your life that is greater than the mistake you've made, or the tragedy that has struck you, or the loss you have suffered.

Start giving of *yourself*. Pour your time, your energy, your money, your love, your ideas into something, and do it as to the Lord. Give it as a seed of your faith which God will use to change your loss and replace it with an equal benefit. Remember, God is the God of a second chance, but you've got to plant your seed first.

Consider

1. Have you suffered a loss? A tragedy? What seed of equal benefit can you plant?

2. What seeds are available to you right now? A seed of prayer? A seed of forgiveness? A seed of money? A seed of time? A seed of encouraging words?

Open Your Mind
to Revelational Knowledge

If you visit the Oral Roberts University campus in Tulsa, Oklahoma, you won't be here long before you'll come across the name Skrinde. He was a member of the founding board of regents of ORU, and he has blessed the campus with many gifts, including the great organ in Christ's Chapel.

William Skrinde and his wife came to my crusade in Seattle, Washington, when Mr. Skrinde was about seventy years old. He was an inventor, and one of his inventions had been a part for the wheel of the Jeep. He had been unable to sell it, however, and had literally poured out his life and exhausted his supply of money in trying to convince the Jeep manufacturers of the worth of his invention. By the time he came to our crusade he and his wife were living hand-to-mouth. Mr. Skrinde was working in a convalescent home, making about two-hundred dollars a month in addition to their Social Security.

During the crusade, they accepted Christ into their lives and joined with me in a Blessing Pact, planting SEED-FAITH gifts at ten dollars a month. Mr. Skrinde had heard me preach that God will multiply your seed sown. He believed it.

Then during that crusade, the Lord led me to say, "Look for ideas. Go up in your attic. Open your closet doors. Look in your dresser drawers. Look around. There may be something God has there for you that you haven't seen. Be observant. Be expectant."

Mr. Skrinde went home, climbed up into his attic, and found the papers that he had drawn up years before. He looked at them and felt led in his spirit to try one more time with the makers of the Jeep. He was already in a rhythm of planting SEED-FAITH. He was ready for his miracle supply to begin.

And this time, Jeep bought the invention. Mr. Skrinde became rich as a result.

At the time we met Mr. Skrinde, he was stooped over with burdens—not physically, but in his inner man. As he got more and more into the rhythm of planting his seeds of faith and expecting miracles of God, he straightened up on the inside and lived that way until he died at age ninety-two.

Every time I think of Mr. Skrinde, I think of how his life was turned around by the Lord through *revelational knowledge*.

What is revelational knowledge? It is knowledge that begins in your spirit and blossoms in your mind. Mind knowledge begins in your mind and stays there. Someone gives you a fact and you store it, or someone shows you a formula and you learn it. But revelational knowledge is based on the Holy Spirit working in your spirit, filling your being with an overpowering insight into the way God wants things done.

I had an experience with revelational knowledge that I want to share with you. It happened in the early 1960s, just before we began to build Oral Roberts University.

I knew God had called me to "build Him a university and to build it on His authority." I knew that I was called to do it. I had a choice to obey or disobey. I chose to obey. But I didn't know *how* to do it.

I am, first and foremost, an evangelist of the Gospel of Jesus Christ. That is my calling, and it will be until the day I die. I am an ordained minister in my denomination. I preach. I pray for the sick. I have said many times that I feel certain that God called many others who were more qualified than I am to build Him a university, but that for one reason or another, they didn't obey. Finally, God ended up with me, and I chose to obey.

So there I was. I had announced to my partners what God had called me to do. My key associates had called me into a

*Ask God to show you
how to receive
your miracle . . .
the answer you need . . .
the direction you must have.*

*Open your mind
to receiving
His
revelational
knowledge.*

meeting where they had told me they would all resign if I went ahead with building the university. (They thought I was leaving the ministry, especially the healing ministry.) I had told them that if they resigned, so be it, but I was called by God to build Him a university and it would be built. It was a short meeting.

I had no faculty . . . no students . . . no buildings . . . very little money . . . a reluctant staff at first . . . and partners who were willing to help but who really didn't understand all that we were called to do.

Where was I going to begin?

I began by pacing the acreage that we had purchased. I walked the grounds, praying and groaning in my spirit. Over and over and over I walked the acres. I prayed in English. I prayed in my prayer language. And as I prayed and then walked . . . prayed and walked . . . prayed and walked, the Holy Spirit began to flood my spirit with impressions and insights that in turn flooded my mind with ideas about *how* to build the university. I could see in my mind's eye the students coming, the faculty arriving, the library shelves being filled up, the buildings going up. I began to realize what I needed to do first and then second and then third. God was *revealing* Himself to me and showing me the way *He* would build a university.

And that's really what revelational knowledge is—it's what Jesus would do in a situation if He were here on the earth. It's what Jesus would say, how Jesus would act, what Jesus would desire another person to do.

Some people say, "Well, Oral Roberts, God speaks to you. He doesn't speak to me."

I agree with you that God speaks to me. I have learned over the years to know His voice. God doesn't always speak to me in an audible voice, but I know God is speaking. His voice fills my head, my being, so that for the time no other voice can be heard.

But I also believe God speaks to you. He speaks in a way that is right for you and your personality. You may know His voice as you read the Bible, hear a sermon, listen to a song, witness the wonders of God's creation, or meditate in the silence of your heart. But He speaks . . . to you.

How do I know that?

Because God said that He changes not. That means that His personality doesn't change. What He does, He does. And if God ever spoke to anyone, then God speaks to men and women today. If God ever healed anyone, He heals today. If God ever delivered anyone, He delivers people today. It's God's nature to communicate with man, including you. The problem is, Are you listening?

God has an answer for your problem, my friend. He has a solution to your need. He has a way out of this thing that seems to have you trapped. He has a way for you to emerge on the other side of this difficulty in a way that is greater than anything you've ever known.

How can you start to think Jesus' thoughts and act the way Jesus would act in your situation?

First, *spend sufficient time in your Bible* looking for instances that are like the ones you are experiencing. If you need a healing in your body, get your Bible and read about the miracles where Jesus healed the sick.

Read Matthew 8. In that one chapter we read how Jesus healed a leper with the touch of His hand . . . how Jesus spoke the word of healing for a centurion's servant . . . how Jesus touched the hand of Peter's mother and her fever left her . . . how Jesus ministered that same evening in Peter's home and "they brought to Him many who were demon-possessed. And He cast out the spirits with a word, and healed all who were sick" . . . and how Jesus cast out the demons in two men who lived in the country of the Gergesenes. Perhaps there is no greater healing chapter in all the Bible!

If you need a money miracle, read how Jesus commanded even a fish to capture a coin in its mouth so that the fish could be caught when Peter threw his hook into the water and the money could be used to pay their taxes (see Matt. 17:24–27). Read about the miracle of a net-breaking, boat-sinking load of fish that Jesus enabled Peter, James, and John to catch after they had "planted their seed" of loaning Jesus their boat for preaching (see Luke 5:1–10).

Do you need a miracle of provision for your family? Read about how Jesus fed thousands of people from the lunch of just a few loaves and fishes that a little boy gave Jesus as a "seed" in childlike faith (see Mark 6:32–42).

Build up your faith by reading what God has done. And remember, He changes not. He is the same God today to help you.

Second, *ask God to show you His plan and give you His ideas.* Talk to God as you would talk to another person. Let Him know how you feel. Ask God questions. And give God time to answer you. Get quiet in your spirit so that God has an opportunity to be heard!

Speak to God from the deepest levels of your spirit.

Say, "God, I know You know the answer. I know You *are* the answer. Show me what to do. Tell me how to think, what to say, and how to act and when."

When you get into the Word of God until it fills your mind, it opens you up to hear the Spirit of God speak to your heart. Then as you listen, God will give you the specific information you need or its broad outline from which you can gather specific ideas and methods. I personally know He will do this for you *if* you spend time with His Word and it gets into your thinking and believing.

God will also send you the person or the people that you need to help you. You need to be sensitive to the Holy Spirit and His revelational knowledge to recognize those people when they arrive.

In 1964, the year before we opened Oral Roberts University, I was struggling to get the first buildings ready for classes to open, trying to get everything organized and hire the people we needed. One day a wealthy man came to see me. Guess what went through my mind when I heard that he was coming?

I knew he headed a large foundation. I knew we had a great financial need. I thought to myself, *The Lord is really working today!*

Well, the man came in and started telling me about himself. In fact, all he seemed to want to talk about was himself. I couldn't wait for him to shut up so I could say something to him. But he just talked a blue streak. Finally, he paused for a moment, and I started to move in and talk about money. Suddenly, he jumped up, and he almost ran out of the place he was in such a hurry to leave. I had destroyed any hope of financial help. I had killed it dead!

After he left, a little voice inside me—I knew it as God's voice—began to rebuke me. He said, *Boy, you sure messed that one up. You didn't care anything about* him. *You were not concerned about him. You were only concerned about what* you *wanted.*

I felt so low I would have had to reach up to touch bottom. Then another word from God came, *You missed it this time, but I'm going to give you another chance.*

That gave me hope. I knew the best thing I could do with that previous mistake was to give it to God. I sure couldn't give it to anybody else. And I didn't want it myself.

Do you realize what I just said?

When you've made a mess of something, the best thing you can do is to give it to God. Apologize for your mistake. That's a great seed to plant. Ask God to forgive you and to help you avoid making that same mistake again. Planting a seed like this is really the only thing you can do with a mistake so that it gives you any positive result.

In a few days my secretary said, "There is a woman here to see you."

The woman walked in and said, "I've come to help you."

I thought she was there for a job. By this time I was so chastened in my spirit I wouldn't have asked anybody for *anything.* She said, "What can I do to help you?"

I said, "I'm sorry. I don't hire the people in this ministry."

She said, "I'm not here for a job. I am excited about your purpose in opening the university, and I would like to help."

I said, "Who are you?"

She gave me her name, and I recognized her as someone I had heard about. She was more affluent than the fellow who had come before! This thought flashed through my mind: *Oral, if you've ever kept your mouth shut and trusted God, shut up and trust your Source today.*

Then she said, "I want to give something as a memorial to my husband who died recently and left me a large inheritance."

I called my secretary and said, "Call my wife."

Evelyn came to my office, and I introduced the woman to her. Then I said to Evelyn, "She wants to give something to us." When Evelyn heard she was a widow and had a large inheritance, she said, "You are the kind of person people take advantage of, and my husband and I don't do that."

We talked further to her to see how we could help her and asked if we could pray with her. Then we said, "Go back home, and if you feel this way in a week, you come back and we'll offer you a SEED-FAITH project."

She said, "I don't see why I need to go home. I'm ready. I have my checkbook."

We said again, "Go home. Have your attorney check us out. If you feel the same way in seven days, come back."

She no doubt decided we were strange people, but she went home. She told us later that when she got home, she recognized with ever greater certainty that we were the kind of people she wanted to deal with. She did have us checked out, and she came back in seven days. I offered her the project of the cost of excavation for the base of the Prayer Tower. She said she would like to do that as well as give the beautiful tiered gardens that now surround the Prayer Tower at the center of the ORU campus.

I said, "Do you know how much it will cost?"

She said, "No, but I'll take it anyway."

I had a large blackboard in my office, and I wrote the cost on it. It was a large amount. Landscaping four acres of sunken garden would not be inexpensive.

Again she said, "I'll take it." And she wrote a check for part of it. Then she said, "I'll give the rest soon."

As the months went by, this woman became a member of the

ORU Board of Regents. Since then she's taken three additional projects, each one larger than the previous one, without anybody asking her. And to think how I could have driven her away by wanting something from her rather than by wanting it from God—rather than by giving God my best, giving to others, and then waiting on God for His best.

The fourth and greatest thing I can say to you about revelational knowledge is to *give to others but expect from God*.

God may reveal to you what He wants you to do. He may reveal to you how He wants you to do it. But He may not reveal to you *who* He is going to use to help you. When others cross your path, *give* your best to them. Be concerned about their problems, their hurts, their concerns, their lives. Help in whatever ways you can. Expect nothing back from them personally. But do expect from God. Then receive it when God sends it as He surely will. That way when men and women give to you, you can know it is from God.

Revelational knowledge can show you God's methods to help you receive the miracle you need. Revelational knowledge reveals how God is going to work in your situation. Be open to receiving God's ideas and inspiration into your life today!

Consider

1. Have you stopped to ask, *What would Jesus do in my situation?*

2. What stories in the Bible describe a circumstance or situation most like the one you are facing?

3. Have you asked God to *show* you directions to take?

4. When someone comes around you who *can* help you, what ways can you find to *give to* that person rather than to *expect from* him?

Don't Give Up

I recall vividly one time in the very early part of my ministry when I closed my Bible and said, "I'm through."

It was November 1947, just six months after I had launched out into the ministry of healing evangelism. I was preaching a crusade in a city auditorium in Kansas. People were coming from a three-state area. There was a great spirit in the meetings. The people were responding to the invitation to accept Christ as Savior and Lord, and many were receiving healing for their illnesses and problems. There was only one thing wrong—the crusade expenses were not being met.

As we neared the close of the crusade, the money we needed to pay the rent on the auditorium was not in hand, and I became very distressed. There had been times before when Evelyn and I had done without in order to pay the bills in connection with our ministry. I knew it was a habit that God didn't want us to fall into. He wanted to *meet* our needs—both in the ministry and in our personal lives.

The mistake I made this time was to brood and worry instead of look to God, the Source of my total supply. I took our lack of money to be a personal failure of my ability to trust God. I allowed it to develop into a matter that so disturbed me that it totally filled my mind. The more I thought about the rent coming due and not having enough funds on hand to pay it, the more disturbed I became. I felt if I could not trust God for finances, how could I continue to trust Him for souls to be saved and the sick to be healed?

I reasoned, if the Lord had really sent me to the people with a message of His healing and delivering power, and if He expected me to be His instrument, I had every right to expect sufficient funds to be raised to meet the obligations incurred by the ministry. I could not bear to think of closing the crusade and leaving the city with unpaid bills. I decided I would sell every personal thing I owned—my car, clothes, everything if need be—to pay those bills. Anything less was a contradiction of all I was and stood for in integrity and faith.

In spite of my thoughts and decisions, though, nothing changed. The crowds remained large and enthusiastic, the spirit was high, and the results were miraculous. We also fell further behind in the crusade budget with each passing meeting.

One evening I was waiting behind the curtain to be announced to preach. My brother Vaden was standing near me. All at once something broke within me, and I said, "I'm through."

He said, "What's wrong?"

Vaden was the brother closest to me in age. We were almost like twins, and he could tell when I was deeply troubled in my spirit.

I said, "I don't have the faith, and God is not helping me."

He said, "Why, Oral, this is a wonderful crusade! What do you mean?"

I said, "Yes, but we can't pay the bills. You know that Papa always taught us to be honest and pay our bills."

I continued, "Vaden, I've done everything I know to do. I've preached the Gospel and prayed for the sick, and people have come to God. But we can't pay the rent on this building. I can't continue and be honest. I am through. It's all over. I am giving up and going home."

Vaden left and quickly returned with Evelyn. She was as white as a sheet. She knew when I said something, I meant it. And there behind the curtain she put her arms around me and

Don't let guilt,
circumstances,
mistakes,
or
the evil intent of others
trip you up.

The Bible promises that
he who endures
will win.
Don't give up!

said, "Oral, I know it's hard, but you can't quit now. The services are too good, and the people are turning more to the Lord every day."

"Evelyn, you know my vow. You and I both promised God that we would never touch the gold or the glory, but we have to have enough to meet our budget. You know it, and I know it. I have prayed to God, but He hasn't heard me. If I am to continue in this ministry, God will have to meet our needs. If He doesn't, I am going home."

She said, "Oral, why don't you go out there and tell the crowd how you feel? Maybe they will do more."

I said, "No. God knows my needs. If I can't trust Him for this, how can I trust Him for the other things?"

She said, "Aren't you going to preach tonight?"

I said, "No, it's all over."

Both she and Vaden left.

Pretty soon I heard her voice over the loudspeaker as she spoke to the crowd. For a moment it startled me. She had never done this before. In fact, she always said, "When I stand up in front of an audience, my mind sits down." But this time she was really talking.

I looked through the curtains. The people were looking at one another and wondering what the evangelist's wife was doing in the pulpit. I moved over to where I could see as well as hear, and I heard her say:

"Friends, you don't know what it means for me to stand up here tonight in my husband's place. And I am sure you don't know him as I do. He has come here by faith. No one is responsible for the financial needs to be met except him and God. He has preached and prayed for you and your loved ones each evening, but tonight he feels like quitting. Some of you have not realized your responsibility in supporting this ministry. We can't even pay the rent on the building. Whatever you may think of Oral, there is this about him that you must know. He is honest, and if he cannot pay the rent, he will not go on. He will not blame you. He will take it as a sign that God does not want him to continue his ministry and he will stop. I know that God has called him and that he must continue to obey God. I am asking you to help him. Together we can save this ministry tonight."

As she spoke, big tears splashed down her face, and I felt smaller and smaller.

What kind of a man am I, I asked myself, *who would give up when the going gets tough? This is probably a very little trial compared to what I will face in the future.* (Little did I realize at that moment how really big problems can get!)

I heard Evelyn say, "Maybe some of you don't know we are in need. Perhaps you are waiting for my husband to say more about it. He won't say any more about it. Now I'm going to do something I've never done in my life. I want some man here to lend me his hat, and I'm going to take a freewill offering for the rent."

Several men volunteered their hats, and Evelyn selected a big-brimmed black one. She held the hat close to her, bowed her head, and prayed. I could tell she was embarrassed. Still, she would not give up. She was determined to save my ministry.

She said, "All right now. The Lord and you must help us. Not just for people here who have need of healing, but for people in other places and lands. I am coming among you to pass the hat. I ask God to help you do your part and bless you for helping us."

Oh, how small my faith was that night! I didn't expect Evelyn to succeed. It seemed I had swung too far from the shore, and it was time to strike for home. The devil whispered, "Well, you have sure sunk pretty low when you have to let your wife take the offering. It's time you gave up."

Listening to the devil and knowing Evelyn felt like dropping through the floor, I knew I was near total defeat. I actually was blaming God. The truth was that by not understanding God as the Source for my *total* supply, I was letting God down as well as myself.

We only needed three hundred dollars that night, but in my mind it seemed ten times larger.

Suddenly, a man stood up in the audience and asked Evelyn for permission to say a word. He was a Jewish businessman who had been attending the services, and we had enjoyed a meal in his home. He had been deeply impressed with the crusade, and we were praying for him.

He said, "Folks, you all know me, I am not a Christian, but if I ever am, these people [gesturing toward the platform] have what I want. I have some money I owe the Lord. I'm starting this offering with twenty dollars."

Evelyn just stood there and waited. Suddenly, a large red-haired woman stood and said, "I'm ashamed of everyone in this audience and especially myself. I'm the mother of several children. We have lots of needs, and the Lord has helped us get many of these needs met through His servant, Oral Roberts. Now you listen to me; I want every one of you to do what I'm going to do." Then she opened her purse, pulled out a worn dollar bill, put it in the hat, and sat down. In a few moments people were standing and saying, "Mrs. Roberts, bring that hat over here."

As Evelyn went through the crowd, I was thoroughly ashamed of myself. When she had finished with the offering, I finally had the courage to step to the platform. I was conscious that every eye was upon me. I had no idea whether enough had been taken to raise the rent or not. A new feeling was taking possession of me. My wife had done something few wives would have had courage to do for their husbands. I knew also that she had not done this only for me. A team of wild horses could not have pulled her up there. She had willingly gone before the people because she knew that a ministry God had given me was endangered.

The need for the rent money was fully met that night. I knew that it was an answer from God to me personally. It was also a gentle rebuke. When I stepped forward to take over the service, I made no reference to what Evelyn had done. I felt that I could only atone for it by taking my Bible, preaching the Gospel, and praying for the people. I read my text and began to preach. And I tell you, the power of a Niagara Falls seemed to be released in me. I knew that the tide had turned. The crusade ended with a packed house and with the audience standing en masse, urging us to return for another series of meetings.

I am sure that when God gives out the credit for the souls that were saved and the lives that were changed during that crusade, more of the credit will go to Evelyn than to me. *Because Evelyn did not give up.*

I learned several great lessons from that experience. One of them was that it isn't wrong to tell somebody when we are hurting and in need. God works through people. In fact, He doesn't have any other way to work on this earth. He wasn't going to rain money out of the skies for us to pick up from the ground. No. God had led certain people to attend those meetings. They had the means to help pay the rent so that the burden of finances could be lifted. And furthermore, by denying them the opportunity to give, we were actually cheating them out of the opportunity to plant a seed of their faith so God could bless them.

Paul wrote this to the church in Philippi. These people had learned the meaning of giving and receiving, and Paul praised them for it when he wrote to them:

> Now you Philippians know also that in the beginning of the gospel, when I departed from Macedonia, no church shared with me concerning giving and receiving but you only. For even in Thessalonica you sent aid once and again for my necessities. Not that I seek the gift, *but I seek the fruit that abounds to your account* (Phil. 4:15–17, italics added).

No, it is not wrong for us to tell others about the needs we have when we are doing work for the Lord. Our money troubles in that crusade were not my personal problem. They were an attack against the ongoing ministry of Jesus on this earth. And had Evelyn not gone to the people, we would have actually *robbed* them of the opportunity to fight the devil and to plant their seeds of faith so that the Lord might have something to turn into the harvest of miracles they needed.

We must realize that some of the attacks that come against us are coming against our witness for the Lord Jesus Christ. And it isn't wrong to tell our fellow Christians when we are facing that kind of attack. In fact, we are *supposed* to tell others. That is part of being in the *body* of Christ so that we can help one another.

I also learned another lesson from that experience—perhaps the most important one of all: There just isn't any way to get through life without having our very existence threatened.

The fact is that the devil knows where we are vulnerable. He knows our weakest points, and he hits us there. Money, that particular night, was our weakest point. And the devil was striking at the money issue to try to destroy our commitment.

The devil is also determined to keep striking at us. We are in a struggle with the devil that doesn't end. Oh, we may win one round. But we will not win the entire fight until the day we die. We need to know that . . . prepare for it . . . and be ready with our faith when the devil strikes at us.

What am I saying to you? I'm saying that on your road to recovery, you're going to continue to encounter obstacles. The Bible is very clear on that point. But Jesus also promised, "He who *endures to the end* shall be saved" (Matt. 24:13, italics added).

We faced another night that could have destroyed our ministry less than three years later. In September 1950 we took the big tent to Amarillo, Texas. The Amarillo Crusade was a great one. More than twenty-four hundred people were saved. The miracles of healing were outstanding, and the people were moved with the presence and power of the Lord.

On the tenth night of the crusade, a storm struck. The winds came roaring in from the northwest. I was standing at the pulpit when suddenly the lights went out. I shouted, "Everyone stay seated and keep your mind on God!" They did. In the flash of lighting I saw the entire tent begin to lift toward the sky. It looked like billows of light above me. Then it began to settle, floating down slowly.

"Oh, Lord, save the seven-thousand people from harm!" I prayed.

It seemed as if a thousand invisible hands took control of the situation.

I remembered a statement that I had made during one of my sermons earlier in the crusade. I said, "The storms of life come to everybody—to the saved and unsaved, to those who live in God's will and to those who don't. The only difference is that Jesus is in the Christian's boat, just as He was with the apostles [see Luke 8:22–25]. Jesus makes all the difference in the world."

I knew God was riding in our boat that night.

The lightning continued to flash all around us, and the winds began to roar like a freight train. The next thing I knew, the rear of the tent lifted over my head, and I felt myself falling backward. I said, "Lord, this is it."

I was laid down very gently on the lower section of the platform as if by an invisible hand. I still had the microphone in my hands. I was not hurt. Then I heard several hundred people singing. A man near me began to praise the Lord. I climbed back to the main platform which was still intact.

I looked back at the crowd. The aluminum poles were gently lowering toward the people on the chairs. The big one-thousand-pound steel center poles were inching toward the ground. A part of the tent draped over the chairs, and I saw people crawling out from under the tattered tent, fighting canvas off their heads. No one panicked.

Every person came out alive from that experience. About fifty people were slightly hurt, but none seriously.

I ran from group to group, praying with people and praising God for our safety.

Meanwhile the hail was really coming down. People had chairs over their heads to protect them.

The firemen soon arrived and searched through the tent. Then they announced that no one was left under it. A policeman rushed up to me and said, "Reverend Roberts, this is the most miraculous thing I have ever seen."

The newspaper reporters found me. I told them how it happened. One was almost in tears. "Brother Roberts," he said,

"God was there." The next morning the *Amarillo Times* crowded the Korean War news off the front page and ran a blazing headline: ESCAPE OF 7,000 CALLED MIRACLE.

The next morning I went out to see the wreckage. Poles and ripped canvas lay over the chairs. How anybody could have gotten out alive can only be answered by what one of the insurance men said to me, "Reverend Roberts, the good Lord had His hand over this place last night." He was right.

As I stood there surveying the wreckage and wondering again if I was through in the ministry, someone handed me a telegram that was from one of our partners, Jeff Lockharts, in Colorado. It read:

"DEAR BROTHER ROBERTS: YOU CAN'T GO UNDER FOR GOING OVER."

Something leaped in my heart. I looked at the remains of that old tent, and for the first time since the storm, tears came to my eyes. I said, "Old tent, you are gone. But I have no regrets. You fought the battle with me, and thousands of people have come to Jesus Christ under your shelter."

Then I said to the Lord, "Lord, I have no regrets. I had nothing when I started three years ago but faith. I still have that faith. You protected the lives of seven thousand people in the midst of the storm here last night. No sermon I might have preached could compare with this mighty miracle. With Your help, I will begin again. I will secure a *bigger* tent, one that can withstand the storms."

And that is exactly what we did.

I told the people about our plans as I preached on our radio broadcasts. I told them how faith leaped in my heart. I told them how the words of one of my own sermons had come back to me through a telegram: "You can't go under for going over." I told them, "With God's help we're going over."

Vaden and I met with various engineers. We discovered an interesting thing. Up until that time, engineers had not been able to construct a tent that would survive a hundred-mile-an-

179

hour wind. That didn't mean that it *couldn't* be done. It just meant that it *hadn't* been done *yet*. That's a very important point.

Something in your problem may be crying out to you, "It can't be done." Your response should be, "That may *not* be true. Maybe it just *hasn't* been done *yet*."

We finally met with a group of engineers who had come up with a plan for a tent that would withstand the storms. It was much larger than the tent we'd had before.

This new tent could seat twelve thousand people—nearly double what our previous tent could hold.

I went to my partners and shared the challenge with them. Our loss from the previous tent had been $41,450, and only seventy percent of that had been covered by the insurance we had. The new tent was going to be considerably more expensive, but it would also be safer. And I believed it was going to be more effective than our going into community buildings. In those days, the great community convention halls had not yet been built. The largest auditorium in most cities could seat only five thousand people. I laid it all out before my partners.

They responded.

We ordered the tent.

And for the next fifteen years, we used giant Cathedral Tents for our crusade meetings across America. They experienced winds that were even stronger than the Amarillo storm . . . but they were never blown down. And under their shelter, audiences of more than twenty thousand crowded inside and around the outside to hear the Gospel, with as many as two thousand people accepting the Lord Jesus Christ into their lives in a single night.

Friend, the devil may knock you down. But if you don't give up, he can't knock you out.

What the devil means for your harm, God can turn to good!

Perhaps God will exchange your torn, old, battered tent . . . for a *new* tent.

Perhaps God will exchange your little tent . . . for a *bigger* tent.

Perhaps God will exchange your fragile tent . . . for a *stronger*, *better* tent!

Don't give up!

Did our problems stop once we had purchased our big eight-pole tent? Far from it. The miraculous power of God is always a direct frontal attack on the kingdom of Satan. In Australia we saw Satan's counterattack.

It was 1956. A group of ministers representing the Full Gospel Churches, operating under permission of the Australian government, had invited us to hold crusade services. The city fathers of both Sydney and Melbourne granted us the use of their beautiful city parks for out tent. We shipped it to Australia and flew there once it had arrived.

Australia was hungry for God. The people were eager for the meetings that spoke of God's healing and delivering power. The parks were a beautiful natural setting for the great tent and the crusade services.

But . . . apparently acting under the influence of certain political figures, it seemed to me that some of the media in the two cities decided that we would not have successful meetings in Australia. Prewritten stories greeted us as the first crusade opened in Sydney. Later, a few half-truths were sprinkled in—to give the stories the appearance of factual reporting, in my opinion. I was told that one reporter who was reproved by a minister for this travesty said, "We are not writing what we want to write, but what we are told to write."

In spite of this negative influence, more than seventy-five thousand people attended the nine-day crusade. The power of God was witnessed by hundreds who decided to follow Christ. Many testified openly of miraculous healing.

The police cooperated splendidly and instructed our workers in the handling of the large crowds. Order was maintained, and with little exception, the people were reverent. Approximately three thousand people came forward in the ten services to give their hearts to God. Our Australian representative called them "the largest altar calls in Australia's history" to that point.

We moved on to Melbourne.

The meetings there started off on an even larger scale. In fact, it looked as if the opening night might be the greatest opening night of all our crusade services. Twelve thousand people packed the tent. Four hundred came forward for salvation. A nurse who had come hundreds of miles for prayer for her deformed feet was miraculously healed.

The following morning . . . Monday . . . a segment of the media launched what I felt was an all-out attack. It seemed to me that every conceivable ruse was used to mislead the people and keep them away from the meetings.

On Monday night, heckling started during the service. Several people yelled out loudly to interrupt during the preaching and praying for the sick. By Wednesday night, it was obvious to us that the opposition was organized. Hecklers, who came to the front with the converts, yelled and screamed their defiance openly. Several rushed to the platform and spat in my face and tried to move me off the platform. Well-known agitators were recognized moving through the audience. I felt that they were deliberately hindering those who were beginning to move forward to accept Christ. It was then that I realized the mob was not against me. When they hissed at the Word of God and defied sinners to receive Christ as their personal Savior, they were really operating against God.

After the Wednesday service was dismissed, the mob surged to the back of the tent, seemingly to get me. I had already been rushed off the grounds with a police escort, but the angry mob attempted to turn over the car that Evelyn was sitting in, probably because they thought I was in it also. When they found I wasn't, they quit.

Several times Evelyn received phone calls saying, "If you want your husband alive, get him out of Australia because we are going to see that he doesn't live if he stays here." That night one our trucks was set on fire, and one rope of the big tent was cut. The next morning I opened the paper to read this headline:

FIRE SET AT ORAL ROBERTS' TENT . . .

Little did I know when I read that headline that the tent was already dismantled and on its way to the ship.

My close associates had held a prayer meeting around midnight after the meeting had closed. They read Acts 19:30–31, which says,

> And when Paul wanted to go in to the people, the disciples would not allow him. Then some of the officials of Asia, who were his friends, sent to him pleading that he would not venture into the theater.

My associates had taken the matter into their own hands, believing that God was moving through them with the gift of wisdom. The next day they handed me my plane tickets back to America.

On the surface, this may have looked like a defeat. We had not conducted our meetings until their preannounced conclusion. But the real Australian story has a victorious ending.

Our move caught the media by surprise. The full responsibility for the canceled meetings was thrown into the laps of those who had stirred up and supported the mobs. They could not deny their guilt, for all Australia had witnessed their reports. A greater good was that this incident underlined the fact that true religious liberty was not known there, although they *claimed* to have that freedom. It set in motion a drive to get a new law passed to guarantee individual freedom to worship God according to the dictates of one's conscience.

The fact is that we were not the only ones being harassed. Similar mobs had been going into the various churches just as they had come into our tent meetings.

Later, Billy Graham went to Australia for a crusade, and he was able to proceed without such harassment. He wrote me a letter that broke me up and made me weep. He said he'd met people who had been saved and healed in my crusade, and he wanted to encourage me. He was able to hold a great crusade . . . and the people came without fear that they would be harmed by a mob of dissenters.

For years and years after the Australian crusade, we received reports from individuals who were saved or healed in our meetings, as well as from those who were helped through the television, radio, and literature ministries that we maintained in Australia. That's right. We may have brought our tent home, but we kept our office in Australia open. We continued through *other channels* to keep the Gospel message flowing to the people who wanted it and who were in need.

What does this have to do with your life and *your* road to recovery?

Friend, the defeats you may experience along the way may not *be* defeats in God's eyes. The Bible speaks of the Lord's work in this way: "One sows and another reaps" (John 4:37). What we had suffered in Australia opened the way for others to experience great triumphs later.

Also, your *work* may be defeated temporarily, but *you* don't need to be defeated. I didn't stop preaching the Gospel because of what had happened in Australia. Far from it. I didn't stop preaching *in other nations* because of what had happened in Australia. Far from it. We went on to minister in more than forty other nations after that incident in Melbourne.

Your marriage may have been destroyed, but *you* don't need to be defeated. Your business or your farm may have been destroyed, but *you* don't need to be defeated. Your physical body may have taken a blow, but *you* don't need to be defeated. *Don't give up!*

Why have I shared these experiences with you? Because I think they point to three of the most severe ways that you are struck by the devil in your life. You can be struck by lack of money. You can be struck by a natural catastrophe, including sickness. You can be struck by what someone else does to you. All three can be the devil's weapons . . . but none of them has to be fatal.

You can also be struck at the point where you have made a mistake. Or at least the devil would like to convince you that you have made a mistake.

Rebecca is not our only child to have died tragically. Our second child and oldest son, Ronald, also died . . . by his own hand.

There is perhaps no greater moment of feeling like a failure than the moment when a parent hears the news that a child has committed suicide. Ronald's death struck Evelyn and me in a way that was different from Rebecca's death. Rebecca and Marshall had been killed suddenly, without warning, in an exploding airplane, in a terrifying storm. The storm in Ronnie's life had been on the inside. And it seemed that we had watched him die little by little by little over a long period of time.

Ronald was brilliant, gifted in languages and music. He was also a sensitive child. In many ways, the criticism that my ministry suffered during the 1950s affected Rebecca and Ronnie much more than our two later children, Richard and Roberta. Of all the children, Ronnie took the criticism most to heart. When he reached the age for college, he chose Stanford University. But even by going nearly two thousand miles away from home, Ronnie couldn't escape the fact that he was Oral Roberts's son.

He entered the military, and because of his ability with languages, he was sent to translation school. He served with the security division during the Vietnam War, and by the time Ronnie returned home, we knew that something had happened inside him—something that was never able to reverse itself again.

This is not to say that Ronnie didn't know the Lord. I believe he did. He had a great gift for healing, one that I had experienced personally.

For a number of years, I suffered from sinus difficulties. During a prime-time television special we were taping in Hawaii, I was struck in a particularly bad way. None of the prescribed medicines or treatments seemed to work. Finally, Evelyn called Ronnie. As Ronnie prayed for me over the phone, I immediately felt the presence of the Lord shoot through my body and my sinuses. A healing began that made it possible for me to sleep through the night for the first time in weeks.

It seems ironic now, but even with Ronnie's awareness of

God's Word and healing power flowing through him, Ronnie became addicted to a prescription drug. As the years went by, that addiction became stronger and stronger. To maintain his addiction, his need for money became greater and greater. His marriage began to fall apart, as did his business. His judgment failed—first in little things and then in bigger things.

Evelyn and I did everything we knew to do. We talked with him . . . prayed with him . . . and not more than three weeks before Ronnie died, we were on our knees with him, holding him and crying before the Lord. We knew that night that Ronnie had experienced a great peace with the Lord, and we believed that the downward spiral of his life would begin to turn upward. Then just a matter of weeks later, the news came that Ronnie was dead.

In the pain of our grief, the devil began to speak to us. "You didn't raise Ronnie right. You were gone from home too much. You shouldn't have been so controversial. You should have been able to help him. After all, you claim to be a minister of the Gospel, and you couldn't help your own son?"

Have such accusations come against you from the devil in the midst of your problem or need?

Well, there are some times when you have to speak right back.

"Devil, Evelyn and I *did* raise Ronnie to serve the Lord. We did teach him the Word of God. We did take him to church regularly. Ronnie was thirty-six years old. He was an adult.

"Devil, Evelyn and I *did* what God asked us to do. You can't make us feel guilty for following the Lord to the best of our ability every day and year of our lives.

"Devil, Evelyn and I did our best to help Ronnie. We did all that we as parents could do.

"Devil, you take this guilt trip off us. We don't deserve it. Take your hands off God's property . . . us!"

That doesn't mean that Evelyn and I didn't grieve for Ronnie. We did. It didn't mean that we refused to acknowledge him as our son or that we tried to hide what happened.

It did mean that we refused to let guilt overwhelm us. We

refused to let a mistake in our lives keep us from facing our future.

Soon after Ronnie died, I felt impressed that I was to read the New Testament on cassette tape *and* to give my life's teachings after each passage I read.

When I told Evelyn about it, I said, "Evelyn, honey, you'll have to help with the recording."

She said, "I can't."

I said, "You've got to."

She said, "You don't understand how I feel. I can't take on a big project like that."

I said, "Evelyn, we've got to work our way out of this grief. The best thing we can do is to plant a seed by reading and teaching the Word of God. I need you to help with the recording so we don't need to go to a big studio somewhere."

Finally, she agreed.

And along with all my other work, day after day, week after week, month after month—for nearly two years, Evelyn and I worked together recording the New Testament.

It was like cold water on our parched souls. The words of Jesus became alive again in the areas of our lives that were numb with grief and pain. As we shared what we had learned about healing . . . as we read the healing words of Jesus . . . as we prayed on the tape for the healing of people . . . a healing was beginning to come back into our own lives.

We dedicated that project to help with cancer research at the City of Faith Health-Care Center—we were planting seed for an even greater healing than our own!

And day after day . . . day after day . . . day after day . . . we came through our grief. We overcame the guilt the devil tried to lay on us. We were healed. We recovered!

Friend, when a mistake or guilt tries to overtake your life . . . *don't give up!*

Find a way to give to others, even when the night seems the darkest. Find something you can *do* that will help other people. And then do it. Do a little each day. Don't give up. Work at it step . . . by step . . . by step . . . by step. Don't become discouraged at the big picture. Be encouraged at the step you make that day!

And I guarantee you, you'll come through it in a way that's greater than you could ever imagine while you were in the midst of your problem.

More than three hundred thousand families ordered the cassette tapes Evelyn and I had prepared on the New Testament. We are still receiving requests for them. And thousands upon thousands of people have written to us telling us how much more they understand about God and His plan for their lives. People have been saved . . . and healed . . . and delivered just by hearing the words of Jesus read aloud to them. Their faith has been built up. Their lives have been turned around.

The Bible tells how Paul escaped with his life one night shortly after his conversion experience on the road to Damascus. Saul—as he was known east of Asia Minor—had been a great enemy of the early church. He had consented to the death of Stephen, the first Christian martyr, and had actually stood by as he died.

Then when he encountered the living Christ in a blinding light as he traveled to Damascus, Saul was dramatically and soundly converted to Christ. Although he was blinded, he was led to Damascus where Ananias, a lay leader in the church there, came to pray for him that his sight might be restored.

Saul remained for some time with the believers in Damascus, learning from them. These were the very people Saul had set out to persecute, and now he was one of them. Soon those Jews who had sponsored Saul on his persecution mission to Damascus began to hear reports that Saul was preaching Christ as the Son of God to the people.

They took counsel to kill Saul, and they sent people to watch the gates of the city day and night. They hoped to ambush Saul as soon as he left the city.

The disciples, however, learned of the plot, and by night they put Saul in a basket and let him down over the wall. He fled into the wilderness, where he continued to grow strong in his faith.

Can you imagine how those disciples felt as they held onto the ropes that were attached to the basket carrying Saul? Surely, they must have wondered about this man who was on the end of the rope.

Can you imagine how Saul must have felt as he was being let down carefully, slowly, into the darkness outside the safety of the city wall? Can you imagine how he wondered at every movement in the darkness below him?

Friend, are you holding the rope for someone today? Are you holding the rope for a situation in your life—believing that it's about to turn around?

Let me encourage you today.

You don't know how close your basket is to touching ground. You may be only inches away from the answer you need.

Hang on.

Don't give up!

Consider

1. What has come against you to try to discourage you into giving up your dream, giving up your call of God, giving up your goals?

2. Have you shared your difficulty with anyone else or are you trying to carry the burden alone?

3. Can you see the difference between your *work* being defeated and *you* being defeated?

4. Are feelings of guilt causing you to feel like a failure—to feel that nothing you do will ever be right? What is the response to those feelings that Jesus wants you to have?

God Wants You Healed—And So Do I!

Let me encourage you with these words that we use in our television ministry every week:

God wants you healed—and so do I!

Friend, God wants you to recover. He wants you to enter wholeness. I'm as sure of that as I am of my own name.

I want you to recover.

I believe you *can* recover and have something *good* happen in your life that will so overshadow the negative things that you will hardly be able to recall how devastated you once felt.

You can recover . . . if you don't give up.

You can learn to trust God as your Source for every area of your life . . . if you don't give up.

You can decide specifically what you're believing for and then receive it . . . if you don't give up.

You can trade in your bad attitudes and replace them with good ones . . . if you don't give up.

You can choose your Point of Contact and have it work to bring you the miracle you need . . . if you don't give up.

No matter what strikes you, you can give your way out of the problem. A little at a time, you can give your way to a greater victory . . . a bigger success . . . a stronger relationship . . . a new beginning . . . a more wonderful way to life. You can get into a rhythm of planting seeds of your faith and reaping a harvest of miracles that will become a way of life for the rest of your life . . . if you don't give up.

You can use your FAITH-TALK . . . find God's methods . . . experience revelational knowledge. Don't give up!

You can recover.

You can be *made* whole.

Start today. And don't *ever* give up!

Consider

1. What are the new attitudes you want to learn?

2. What are the specific miracles that you desire in your life?

3. What will be your Point of Contact for releasing your faith?

4. What seeds of your faith will you choose to plant?

5. How can you use FAITH-TALK as you expect God's miracles to come into your life?

6. How can you open your life to more revelational knowledge?

7. Is it possible that *endurance* is your number-one key to full recovery?

*Say it often
to yourself:*

*Recovery is
possible!
I can be made
whole!*